בראשית

Bereshit

Shabbat Morning Edition

Elliott Michaelson
MAJS

Copyright Information

PARASHAT BERESHIT

Vital Statistics	
Full text reference:	*Genesis / Bereshit 1: 1 to 6:8*
The *Maftir* reading:	*Genesis / Bereshit 6: 5-8*
Text reference for the Haftarah:	*Isaiah / Yish'ayah 42: 5 to 43: 10 or 42: 5-21*
Special Haftarah for Mahar Hodesh	
(substitute the weekly Haftarah with this one when Shabbat falls on the day before the New Month)	
I Shemu'el / I Samuel 20: 18-42	
Note: the English retelling of the Torah is for the entire *parashah*, not just the *maftir*. The English for the *maftir* consists of the last part of the retelling.	

MY PROGRESS

Date					
Torah blessings					
Torah reading					
Torah review in English					
Haftarah blessings					
Haftarah reading					
Haftarah review in English					

Date					
Torah blessings					
Torah reading					
Torah review in English					
Haftarah blessings					
Haftarah reading					
Haftarah review in English					

BEFORE YOU BEGIN: GOOD THINGS TO ASK ABOUT THIS BOOK

Welcome to your Bar/Bat Mitzvah Survival Guide! There are some unique features about this guide that might be useful to you during your studies, such as...

What's up with the names of people and places?

Brace yourself, for what I'm about to say (or write, actually) may come as a shock. THE TORAH IS WRITTEN IN HEBREW. Big surprise, I know. So here's the issue many of my students have: in English, we call him *Moses* but in the Torah, we call him *Moshe*. The first woman on Earth is called *Eve* but in Hebrew, she's called *Hava*. The Jews were slaves in *Egypt* — or was it *Mitzra'im*? The answer is both. To try to avoid this confusion between English and Hebrew names, I've decided to stick with the Hebrew. So מֹשֶׁה is translated as *Moshe*, not *Moses*, and יְרוּשָׁלַיִם is *Yerushalayim*, not *Jerusalem*. For more on how to pronounce the Hebrew names, check out the handy translation chart on page ten.

How do you show God talking?

Many of us think of God as an inspirational force in our lives, but how many of us have actual physical conversations with God? As a kid, I was always confused by the fact that God physically speaks to people in the Torah but not to us today. When the Torah records God's "speech", we don't have to think of it as physical words all the time. Moses Maimonides was one of the greatest philosophers and teachers in Judaism, and 800 years ago he famously taught that all divine language in the Torah is metaphorical. Taking that to heart, I've done my very best to express that in my English retellings. God's "dialogue" is written in a different font and with a different tone, and I avoid using direct language like "said" or "told". So did Avraham hear the actual voice of God, or did God act as Avraham's inspirational inner voice? Both beliefs are valid, and it's something I encourage you to explore with your family and your teacher / rabbi.

In these retellings, I refer to God by two proper nouns: *Adonai* and *Elohim*. *Adonai* is God's actual, personal name: י-ה-ו-ה. You'll find it all over the place in the Tanah and in many sidurim. *Elohim* (אֱלֹהִים) is the Hebrew word for "God". Since the Tanah uses both as personal names for God, I've decided to keep the proper Hebrew terms.

What about commentary and translation?

Judaism has always accepted that the Torah text contains four layers of understanding. There's the literal, basic text that you see in front of you (peshat), but underneath the basic text are three layers of metaphorical understanding just waiting to be discovered (derash, remez, sod). You have over two thousand years of scholarship and commentary — including some great stuff being written today — to help you discover these hidden meanings. I've deliberately avoided providing them here for one all-important reason: any commentaries I select would reflect *my* perspective on the text and how it should be taught, and I want you to be free to find *your own way*. That's why I'm leaving the selection of commentary up to you and your rabbi / teacher.

Instead, I've devoted my time to a careful retelling of the Torah and Haftarah texts in English. This isn't a strict translation, but it isn't a sanitized children's version, either. My aim is to provide an English format that flows as easily as a work of juvenile literature, but which preserves the content and significance of the Biblical text. I've also included suggestions for study and analysis that are based on media literacy expectations from public school programs. These blurbs usually address social and historical questions that my own students ask because they need help understanding the ancient society that produced our sacred texts. None of this replaces Rabbinic commentary, but first you need to understand a little bit about the world of our ancient cousins. Then you can work with your rabbi / teacher to find the commentaries that speak to your own interests and concerns.

Da Links!

If you're using the ebook version of this book, try tapping the hyperlinks that appear periodically in the text. Some of them will take you to useful Google maps of many of the locations mentioned in the Torah, while others will take you the *Jewish Virtual Library* or *My Jewish Learning* to learn more about the famous people and nations from the Torah and Haftarah. Enjoy!

-- EM, fall 2015

TRANSLITERATIONS OF HEBREW VOWEL SOUNDS

(A very handy reference guide...)

E

Same sound as:
SPECIAL
THEM
HEAD

* Note that the *Shva* can also indicate the absence of a vowel sound.

O

Same sound as:
HOPE
GROW
BOAT

A

Same sound as:
CUP
TROUBLE
SUPPER

U

Same sound as:
NOODLES
GROUP
SUPER

I

Same sound as:
MEATBALL
PIECE
AGREE

AY

Same sound as:
THEY
AGENT
STEAK

* Some pronounce the *Tzayreh* as "E", some pronounce it as "AY", and some use both pronunciations.

AI

Same sound as:
EYEBALL
RIGHT
LIBRARY

Our *Bar/Bat Mitzvah Survival Guides* use the proper Hebrew names for people and places. The transliterations on this page will help you pronounce them properly. Sometimes, the English and Hebrew names are very close, but often they're quite different. Here are some of the most common differences.

Ashur	Assyria
Bavel	Babylon
Mitzra'im	Egypt
Moshe	Moses
Rivkah	Rebekah
Sha'ul	Saul
Shlomo	Solomon
Ya'akov	Jacob
Yehezk'el	Ezekiel
Yehoshu'a	Joshua
Yehudah	Judah
Yerushalayim	Jerusalem
Yirmiyahu	Jeremiah
Yish'ayah	Isaiah
Yisra'el	Israel
Yitzhak	Isaac
Yosef	Joseph

PUTTING ON THE TALLIT & TEFILLIN

If you've never had the chance to put on the *tallit* or *tefillin*, this is your lucky day! Traditionally, the *tallit* and *tefillin* are worn for all weekday morning services. On Shabbat and Holy Day mornings, only the *tallit* is worn (except Yom Kippur, when we wear the tallit all day). Why the difference? There are many explanations. My favorite reason goes like this: the Torah teaches us to wear reminders of our Divine Agreement with God on our arms and our heads (i.e. *tefillin*). On Shabbat, Pesa<u>h</u>, Shavu'ot, Sukkot, Rosh Hashanah, and Yom Kippur, we perform rituals all day long that remind us of God's Agreement with us, so we don't need the *tefillin* to remind us. To put everything on, follow these basic steps. You can also find a video on our website at **http://www.adventurejudaism.net/Bar_Bat_Mitzvah_Guides.html**.

1

Recite the bra<u>h</u>ah for wrapping yourself in the tallit.

בָּרוּךְ אַתָּה יְיָ אֱלֹהֵינוּ מֶלֶךְ הָעוֹלָם, אֲשֶׁר קִדְּשָׁנוּ בְּמִצְוֹתָיו, וְצִוָּנוּ לְהִתְעַטֵּף בַּצִּיצִת.

We praise You, Adonai our God, Ruler of the universe, whose *mitzvot* make us holy, and who commanded us to cover ourselves with *tzitzit*.

2

Wrap the collar around your shoulders as if you were putting on a cape.

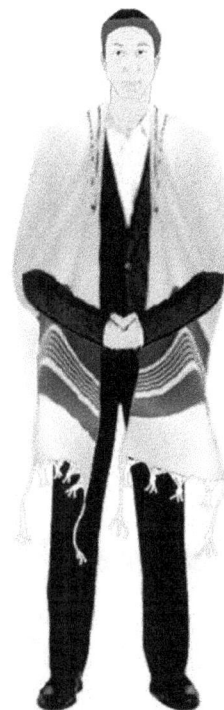

On Shabbat and Holy Day mornings, stop here!

3

Loop the *tefillin shel yad* (the one with the extra-long strap) around your bicep.

If you're left-handed, use your right bicep. If you're right-handed, use your left bicep. If you're ambidextrous like me, take your pick!

4

Before tightening the loop, recite this bra*h*ah.

בָּרוּךְ אַתָּה יְיָ אֱלֹהֵינוּ מֶלֶךְ הָעוֹלָם, אֲשֶׁר קִדְּשָׁנוּ בְּמִצְוֹתָיו, וְצִוָּנוּ לְהָנִיחַ תְּפִלִּין.

We praise You, Adonai our God, Ruler of the universe, whose *mitzvot* make us holy, and who commanded us to put on *tefillin*.

5

Tighten the loop around your bicep and wrap the strap around your forearm 7 times.

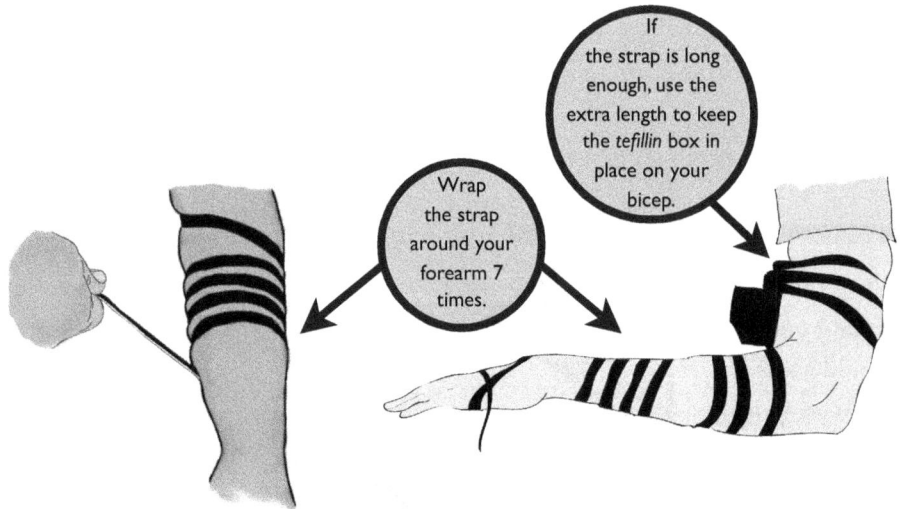

Wrap the strap around your forearm 7 times.

If the strap is long enough, use the extra length to keep the *tefillin* box in place on your bicep.

6

Place the *tefillin shel rosh* at the center of your forehead, right at the hairline.

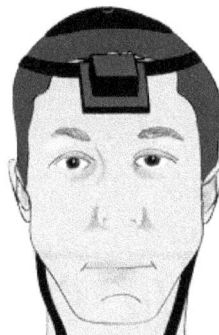

Two long straps extend from the back of the *tefillin shel rosh*. Let them hang freely on either side of your head.

7

Recite the bra<u>h</u>ah for the *tefillin shel rosh*.

בָּרוּךְ אַתָּה יְיָ אֱלֹהֵינוּ מֶלֶךְ הָעוֹלָם, אֲשֶׁר קִדְּשָׁנוּ בְּמִצְוֹתָיו, וְצִוָּנוּ עַל מִצְוַת תְּפִלִּין.

We praise You, Adonai our God, Ruler of the universe, whose *mitzvot* make us holy, and who commanded the *mitzvah* of *tefillin*.

8

Finish wrapping the *tefillin shel yad* by winding it around your middle finger 3 times.

If the strap is long enough, you can also wind it around your hand to help keep everything in place.

Tefillin shel rosh with the two hanging straps.

Tefillin shel yad around the bicep (under the *tallit*.)

Tefillin shel yad wrapped 3 times around the middle finger.

Tefillin shel yad wrapped 7 times around the forearm.

You're ready to go! When you're finished, take everything off in the reverse order.

THE WEEKLY PARASHAH AND HAFTARAH

TORAH IN ENGLISH: BERESHIT / GENESIS 1: 1 TO 6: 8

What's the story so far?

Okay, you got me. How can there be a "story so far" if this is the first parashah in the Torah? Good question. One answer is that the Torah has no start or finish. We read it in a cycle, so that when we reach the last parashah we immediately rewind and start again with the first parashah. Since we read the whole Torah every year, when we read *Bereshit*, we make connections to what we know happens later on. For example, when we read about the separation of Shabbat as a day of rest at the end of Creation, the Torah expects us to connect this to mitzvot in later books that outline the observance of Shabbat. When we read about the laws of Shabbat later on (say, in the Ten Commandments), we're expected to make connections to events in *Bereshit*.

What can I expect from this parashah?

There's a lot going on in *Bereshit*. God creates everything (twice); the first human beings are placed in Eden; they eat from the forbidden tree and are severely punished & exiled; one of their sons kills the other following a mysterious argument; humanity spreads out across the earth and fills the world with corruption. The parashah ends ominously with God regretting the act of Creation.

Much of *Bereshit* is hard to accept at face value, and people who treat the Torah like a science textbook are going to be disappointed. You won't find any support for scientific theories like Big Bang, Evolution, or Natural Selection to explain how the world came to be and how life began. That's because Science is about human inspiration and observation, but Torah study is about divine inspiration. In other words, Science tells us how the universe works; Torah teaches us what the universe's workings mean for us as human beings. Keep this in mind as you read through the parashah.

And so, without further ado, on to the Torah...

CREATION

> 1: 1-5
> The Shabbat pm /
> Weekday Torah
> reading starts here.

When Elohim began creating the heavens and the earth, the earth had no shape or form, and everything was in darkness and chaos. Elohim's spirit swept over the water.

Let there be light!

There was light. Elohim saw that this was good. Elohim separated Light from Darkness to make the first Day and Night.

Evening and morning passed for the First Day.

> **When Elohim began creating:** How can the Torah say that the world was created in six days when everything we know about science says otherwise? The Torah is a book of *religion*, not *science*. Science explains how the universe works. Religion teaches us what the universe's workings *mean* to us as human beings. Think of it this way: your science textbook uses theories like Evolution and Natural Selection to explain how human beings came to exist as we are today. The Torah (and 3000 years of prophets and rabbis) teaches us about the moral and ethical responsibilities that come with being human. As you read through the rest of *Bereshit*, think about the difference between religion and science. Think *metaphorically*, not *literally*.

> 1: 6-8

Let there be a division to separate the water!

It happened. Elohim separated the water, placing some of it above the division and some of it below. Elohim called the division "Sky". Evening and morning passed for the Second Day.

> 1: 9-13
> The Shabbat pm /
> Weekday Torah
> reading ends at vs. 13.

Let the water under the sky be gathered into one place so that dry areas can be seen!

It happened. Elohim called the dry areas "Land", and the areas with water Elohim called "Seas". Elohim saw that this was good.

Let the land grow mature plant life with ripe seeds and fruit!

It happened. The land grew mature plants of every kind. Seeing this, Elohim felt good. Evening and morning passed for the Third Day.

1: 14-19

Let there be lights in the Sky to distinguish between Day and Night, and to allow festivals, days, and years to be marked off. Let these lights illuminate the Land!

It happened. Elohim assembled the two largest lights: the greater one to illuminate Day and the smaller one to illuminate Night, along with the stars. Elohim placed them in the Sky to provide light for the Land and to separate Day and Night.
Elohim saw that this was good. Evening and morning passed for the Fourth Day.

1: 20-23

Let the Sea fill with animal life, and let the Land fill with birds that fly across the Sky!

Elohim created the largest sea creatures and all the other species of animal life that fill the Sea, along with every species of bird. Elohim saw that this was good, and blessed them.

Be fruitful, have many offspring, and fill the Sea and the Land!

Evening and morning passed for the Fifth Day.

1: 24-28

Let the Land produce every species of roaming animal, insect, and everything that crawls on the ground.

It happened. Elohim made every species of roaming animal, insect, and everything that crawls. Elohim saw that this was good.

Let Us make Humans in Our image, to be like Us. They will take charge of the animals in the Sea, the birds of the Sky, and all the creatures that live on the Land.

Elohim created Humans in Elohim's image, and made male and female together. Elohim blessed them.

1:28-31

Be fruitful, have many offspring, fill the Land, and be in command over it. Take charge of the animals in the Sea, the birds of the Sky, and all the creatures that live on the Land. For food, I give you the grasses of the field and the fruit trees. To the birds of the Sky and the creatures on the Land, I give all forms of vegetation to eat.

Elohim created humans...: Human beings are arguably the most powerful creatures on Earth (at least, we like to think we are). So why do you think the Torah says that we were created last — shouldn't we have come first? If everything was here before we were, what might this say about our role in the world? How does this affect your understanding of God's blessing in the next paragraph?

And what's this about being created in God's image? God has no physical shape. How can you be created in the image of something that has no shape? Hint: the word "image" has more than one meaning. Keep this metaphor in mind as you continue reading the Eden story...

Elohim saw everything that had been accomplished, and it was very good. Evening and morning passed for the Sixth Day.

EDEN

2:1-3

The creation of heaven, earth, and everything in them was now complete. By the Seventh Day, all the labor was done, and Elohim rested from the effort. Since this was the day of rest from all the creative work that Elohim set out to do, Elohim blessed the Seventh Day and made it holy.

2:4-9

*HERE IS THE **HISTORY OF THE CREATION OF HEAVEN AND EARTH** ON THE DAY THEY WERE MADE BY ADONAI ELOHIM...*

History of the creation of heaven and earth: Here we see a second Creation story. How does this one compare with the previous one? Remember that the Torah is a book of *religion*, not *science*. Explore the moral lessons embedded in this story. Remember: think metaphorically!

There wasn't any vegetation on the land because Adonai hadn't yet caused the rain to fall, nor was there any human to till the soil. There was only a mist that welled out of the earth to moisten the ground. Adonai Elohim molded a man out of the dust on the ground, breathed a soul into his nostrils, and brought him to life. Adonai Elohim planted a garden in Eden — in the East — and put the man there. Adonai Elohim caused all kinds of trees to grow that are good for eating, along with the Tree of Life and the Tree of Knowledge of Good and Evil.

2: 10-14

A stream flows out of Eden to water the garden, and it splits into the headwaters of four rivers. The first is called Pishon, and it winds around the land of Ḥavilah where the gold is (the gold there is of good quality, and so are the bdellium and lapis-lazuli.) The second river is called Giḥon, and it winds around the land of Cush. The third river is called Ḥidekel, and it runs east of **Ashur**. The fourth river is called **Ferat**.

Ashur: This is the ancient kingdom of Assyria.

Ferat: The name "Ferat" is Hebrew for the Euphrates, which flows through modern-day Iraq and Syria.

2: 15-25

Adonai Elohim put the man in the garden of Eden to till it and to protect it.

You will eat from any tree in this garden except the Tree of Knowledge of Good and Evil.
On the day you eat from that tree, YOU WILL DIE.

Adonai Elohim considered the man.

It is not proper for the man to be alone. I will make a counterpart for him to help him.

Adonai Elohim molded from the ground all the animals of the field and the birds of the sky, and brought them to the man to see what the man would call them. Whatever the man called them would be

Tree of Knowledge...: Think about what you know about how people behave. Why *wouldn't* God want humanity to know about Good and Evil? Explore the consequences of having this knowledge?

their name. The man gave names to all the animals and the birds, but he didn't find a counterpart to help him. So Adonai Elohim put the man into a deep sleep. While the man slept, Adonai Elohim removed one of his ribs and sealed the wound. Adonai Elohim used the rib to make a woman and brought her to the man.

When the man saw her, he announced, "Finally, someone who's the bone from my bones and the flesh from my flesh! I will call her **'Woman' since she was taken from 'Man'.**"

'Woman'...: This is a pun on the Hebrew words for man (אִישׁ) and woman (אִשָּׁה).

This is why a man leaves his father and mother to bond with his wife — as if they're one flesh.

The man and his woman were naked, but they weren't ashamed about it.

EXILE FROM PARADISE

3: 1-7

Of all the animals created by Adonai Elohim, the snake was the most mischievous. "Did Elohim really tell you not to eat from any tree in the garden?" he asked the woman.

"No, we can eat from any fruit tree in the garden," she replied. "It was only the tree in the center of the garden that Elohim told us not to eat from. We can't even to touch it or we'll die."

"You *won't* die," argued the snake. "Elohim knows that the moment you eat from it, your inner awareness will open and you'll be like Elohim — knowing Good from Evil."

The woman gazed longingly at the tree. She saw that the fruit looked very delicious and that it would make her wise, so she took one and ate it. Then she gave one to her husband and he ate it, too. Suddenly, their inner awareness opened and they realized that they were naked. Sewing together some fig leaves, they made crude underwear.

3: 8-19

As evening came, they felt Adonai Elohim's presence blowing through the garden. The man and woman hid themselves among the trees.

Where are you?

"We felt Your Presence in the garden," stammered the man. "We realized we were naked, so we hid."

Who said you that you were naked? You have eaten from the tree, have you not — the one I told you not to eat from!

The man trembled. "It was the woman You created to be with me! She brought me the fruit and I ate it!"

The woman felt Adonai Elohim's presence directed at her.

What have you done?

"It was the snake," cried the woman. "He tricked me into eating it!"

Because you did this, Snake, you will be cursed among all living things. You are doomed to crawl on your belly and eat dirt for all the days of your life. There will be hatred between you and the woman, and between your descendants and hers. They will strike at your head, and you will strike at their heel.

As for you, Woman, the labors of childbirth will be multiplied, and you will give birth in great pain. You will long for your man, and he will dominate you.

And you, Man: you listened to your wife when she gave you the fruit to eat — after I commanded you not to eat from the tree! The ground will be cursed because of you. Only through hard labor will you benefit from it, though it will produce weeds and thorns, and you will eat only from the grasses of the field. Only by the sweat of your brow will you have bread to eat until the day you return to the earth. You are dust, and to dust you will return!

> Okay, so the man and the woman had one simple rule to follow, and they couldn't even manage to do that. Joking aside, consider the lesson here. What is the Torah trying to teach us about human behavior? How does this event compare to other moments of disobedience and punishment later on in the Torah? How does it compare with the message about disobedience, punishment, and forgiveness in the Haftarah?

3: 20-23

The man named his wife **Hava because she was the mother of all living things**, and Adonai Elohim provided clothes for them made from animal skins.

By knowing Good and Evil, humans have now become like one of Us. They have only to stretch out a hand to the Tree of Life and eat the fruit. Then they will live forever!

> **Hava...:** In Hebrew, her name is חַוָּה, which is usually translated as "Eve". חַוָּה is related to the word חַי, which means "life".

Adonai Elohim exiled the humans from the garden of Eden, where the man now had to till the ground from which he was taken. Having banished them, Adonai Elohim set the **Keruvim** and a spinning, flaming sword to guard the garden of Eden — and the way to the Tree of Life — from the East.

> **Keruvim:** These were mythical winged creatures with human and animal features. The Tanah (Jewish Bible) isn't entirely clear as to exactly what Keruvim looked like, but our ancestors certainly knew. During the time of Moshe (Moses), the top of the Aron (the chest where the first mitzvot were kept) was decorated with two golden Keruvim.

FIRST KILL

The story of humanity's first kill has troubled readers for thousands of years. Like the rest of the events in this parashah, reflect on this metaphorically, not just literally. What moral lessons are embedded here?

4: 1-7

The man slept with his wife, Ḥava. She became pregnant and gave birth to **Kayin**. Explaining the meaning of his name, she said, "I have gotten a man from Adonai." She then gave birth to his brother, **Hevel**. Hevel became a shepherd while Kayin became a farmer.

Time passed. Kayin brought an offering to Adonai from his crops, and Hevel brought the best of his flock's first-born. Adonai acknowledged Hevel and his offering, but Adonai did not acknowledge Kayin and his offering. Kayin turned away in rage.

Kayin: In Hebrew, קַיִן is connected to the phrase "I have gotten" (קָנִיתִי).

Hevel: In Hebrew, הֶבֶל means "breath" or "vapor", though the Torah doesn't provide a reason for his name.

Why are you furious, and why hide your face? Surely, if you do Good, you will be uplifted. But if you do not, evil deeds will lurk at the door. You will feel their urges, but you can master them.

4: 8-15

Kayin spoke to his brother, Hevel. When they were out in the field, Kayin attacked his brother and killed him.

Where is your brother Hevel?

Responding to Adonai's Presence, Kayin answered, "I don't know. Am I my brother's guardian?"

What have you done? Your brother's blood cries out to Me from the ground! You are cursed from the ground, which opened its mouth to take your brother's blood from your hands! When you farm the land, it will no longer give its crop to you. You shall wander the earth forever!

Distraught, Kayin cried out to Adonai, "My punishment is too severe! You've exiled me from the land, and I'll have to hide myself from You. As a wanderer, anyone who sees me might kill me!"

My vengeance shall be seven times greater on whomever kills Kayin!

Adonai placed a mark on Kayin as a warning about the curse to anyone who might attack him.

4: 16-24

Kayin left Adonai's Presence and settled in the land of Nod, which is east of Eden. He slept with his wife, she became pregnant, and gave birth to Hanoh. Kayin built a city and named it after his son. When Hanoh grew up, he had a son named Irad. Irad had a son named Mehuya'el, who in turn had a son named Metusha'el. Metusha'el's son was Lameh.

Lameh had two wives: Adah and Tzillah. Adah gave birth to Yavval, who is the ancestor of people who live among their herds in tents. His brother's name was Yuvval, and he is the ancestor of musicians who play the lyre and the pipe. Tzillah also had children. She gave birth to Tuvval-Kayin, who made all kinds of copper and iron tools. Tuvval-Kayin's sister was Na'amah.

One day, **Lameh announced to his wives**: "Listen to what I have to say! I killed a man who wounded me and a boy who bruised me. If the vengeance on Kayin is seven times greater, mine will be seventy-seven!"

> **Lameh announced...:** What does this mini-story have to do with the main story of Adam and Hava? Not much. The Torah has several mini-stories like this that don't seem to go anywhere. At one time, many centuries ago, this story may have been complete. Who knows how many other ancient Jewish traditions have been lost to time...?

4: 25-26

Adam slept with his wife again. She had a son and called him **Shet**. She explained the meaning of his name: "Elohim has provided me with another child in place of Hevel, who was killed by Kayin." When Shet grew up, he had a son of his own named Enosh. It was at that time when people began to pray to Adonai by name.

> **Adam:** The Hebrew name אָדָם means "human". The word הָאָדָם means "the man". The end of Chapter 4 is the first time when the Torah uses אָדָם as a proper name.
>
> **Shet:** The Hebrew שֵׁת is connected to the phrase "provided me with..." (שָׁת-לִי).

FILLING THE LAND

> 5: 1-20

THIS IS THE BOOK OF THE HISTORY OF HUMANITY...

On the day they were created by Elohim, they were made in Elohim's image — male and female. Elohim blessed them and called them "humans". When Adam was 130 years old, he had a son in his own image named Shet. After Shet was born, Adam lived for another 800 years, and he had more sons and daughters in that time. Adam died at the age of 930.

> What's the point of this exhaustive family tree? The Torah isn't only concerned with teaching us about positive behavior and religion. It's also concerned about teaching us history. Not *scientific* history with archeologists and old relics, but the memory of *oral* history. Our ancient cousins were very interested in remembering where they came from and how different people came to be. Preserving this knowledge was very important to them. Why might this be? How do we benefit today from knowing our family histories? Discuss your ideas!

When Shet was 105, he had a son named Enosh. Shet lived for another 807 years, and he had more sons and daughters. Shet died at the age of 912. When Enosh was 90, he had Kaynan. Enosh lived for another 815 years, and he had more sons and daughters. Enosh died at the age of 905. When Kaynan was 70, he had Mahalal'el. Kaynan lived for another 840 years, had more sons and daughters, and died at the age of 910. Mahalal'el was 65 years old when he had Yared. Mahalal'el lived for another 830 years, had more sons and daughters, and died at the age of 895. When Yared was 162 years old, he had Hanoh. Yared lived another 800 years, had more sons and daughters, and died at the age of 962.

> 5: 21-32

When Hanoh was 65 years old, he had Metushalah. After Metushalah's birth, Hanoh walked with Elohim for 300 years, and had more sons and daughters. Hanoh lived for 365 years. He walked with Elohim, but he disappeared — for Elohim took him.

When Metushalah was 187, he had Lameh. Metushalah lived for another 782 years, had more sons and daughters, and died at the age of 969.

When Lameh was 182, he had a son whom he named No'ah. Lameh explained No'ah's name: "This child will give us relief from our hard work and manual labor on the ground that Adonai cursed." Lameh lived for another 595 years and had more sons and daughters. He died at the age of 777.

> **No'ah:** The Hebrew נֹחַ is connected to the phrase "will give us relief / comfort" (יְנַחֲמֵנוּ).

When No'ah was 500 years old, he had Shem, Ham, and Yafet.

ELOHIM'S REGRET

> 6: 1-4

When the human population increased across the earth, they had many daughters. Elohim's divine followers saw how beautiful they were, and they took any of the daughters they wanted to be their wives.

My breath will not last in humanity forever, for they are made of flesh. Let their lifespan be 120 years!

Elohim's divine followers had children with humanity's daughters. These children were called "Nefilim". These were the heroes of ancient legend.

> 6: 5-8
> This is the Maftir.

Adonai witnessed humanity's great evil in the world. Every desire in their hearts was always wicked. With great sorrow, Adonai regretted making humans.

Adonai witnessed humanity's great evil...: What a great cliffhanger! Cue the ominous music. Of course, our ancient cousins who first read this (or heard it) already knew what comes next, and so should we. But apart from the desire for a good ending, what might the earliest rabbis be trying to teach us by closing the parashah here? Explore the connection between God's decisions here and in the garden of Eden. Compare this with Yish'ayah's attitude to disobedience and punishment in the Haftarah.

I shall wipe out the humans I have made from the face of the earth and every living creature with them.

Only No'ah was acceptable to Adonai.

Up next...

No'ah! God approaches the only righteous man in this horrid generation worth saving: No'ah. The scheme to wipe out and restart all life on earth is hatched as No'ah builds an enormous boat to save two of every species from destruction. When it's all over, God makes a commitment to never again wipe out all life... At least, not with a flood. No'ah's sons have many descendants, and apart from a few slip-ups (notably, a certain babbling tower), manage to thrive. The parashah ends by zeroing in on one of No'ah's descendants — a rather famous individual whom God chooses to be the father of a great nation.

The Maftir and its Blessings (Bereshit 6: 5-8)

Before the Torah reading, recite one of the following blessings.
Your Rabbi or teacher will tell you which one is appropriate for your community.

You call out:

בָּרְכוּ אֶת יְיָ הַמְבֹרָךְ.

The congregation responds:

בָּרוּךְ יְיָ הַמְבֹרָךְ לְעוֹלָם וָעֶד.

You say it back to them:

בָּרוּךְ יְיָ הַמְבֹרָךְ לְעוֹלָם וָעֶד.

You continue:

בָּרוּךְ אַתָּה יְיָ אֱלֹהֵינוּ מֶלֶךְ הָעוֹלָם,

אֲשֶׁר קֵרְבָנוּ לַעֲבוֹדָתוֹ

וְנָתַן לָנוּ אֶת תּוֹרָתוֹ.

בָּרוּךְ אַתָּה יְיָ, נוֹתֵן הַתּוֹרָה.

Let us praise Adonai,
the Blessed One!

Let Adonai, the Blessed One,
be praised forever!

We praise You, Adonai our God,
Ruler of the universe,
Who drew us close to God's Work
and gave us God's Torah.

We praise You, Adonai,
the Giver of Torah.

You call out:

בָּרְכוּ אֶת יְיָ הַמְבֹרָךְ.

The congregation responds:

בָּרוּךְ יְיָ הַמְבֹרָךְ לְעוֹלָם וָעֶד.

You say it back to them:

בָּרוּךְ יְיָ הַמְבֹרָךְ לְעוֹלָם וָעֶד.

You continue:

בָּרוּךְ אַתָּה יְיָ אֱלֹהֵינוּ מֶלֶךְ הָעוֹלָם,

אֲשֶׁר בָּחַר בָּנוּ מִכָּל הָעַמִּים

וְנָתַן לָנוּ אֶת תּוֹרָתוֹ.

בָּרוּךְ אַתָּה יְיָ, נוֹתֵן הַתּוֹרָה.

Let us praise Adonai,
the Blessed One!

Let Adonai, the Blessed One,
be praised forever!

We praise You, Adonai our God,
Ruler of the universe,
Who chose us from all the nations
to be given God's Torah.

We praise You, Adonai,
the Giver of Torah.

מאה ועשרים שׁנה הנפלים היו בארץ
בימים ההם וגם אחרי כן אשר יבאו
בני האלהים אל בנות האדם וילדו
להם המה הגברים אשר מעולם
אנשי השם
וירא יהוה כי רבה רעת האדם בארץ
וכל יצר מחשבת לבו רק רע כל
היום וינחם יהוה כי עשה את האדם
בארץ ויתעצב אל לבו ויאמר יהוה
אמחה את האדם אשר בראתי מעל
פני האדמה מאדם עד בהמה עד
רמש ועד עוף השמים כי נחמתי כי
עשיתם ונח מצא חן בעיני יהוה
אלה תולדת נח נח איש צדיק תמים
היה בדרתיו את האלהים התהלך נח
ויולד נח שלשה בנים את שם את

5. וַיַּרְא יְהֹוָה

כִּי רַבָּה

רָעַת הָאָדָם בָּאָרֶץ

וְכָל־יֵצֶר מַחְשְׁבֹת לִבּוֹ

רַק רַע כָּל־הַיּוֹם:

6. וַיִּנָּחֶם יְהֹוָה

כִּי־עָשָׂה אֶת־הָאָדָם בָּאָרֶץ

וַיִּתְעַצֵּב אֶל־לִבּוֹ:

7. וַיֹּאמֶר יְהֹוָה

אֶמְחֶה אֶת־הָאָדָם אֲשֶׁר־בָּרָאתִי

מֵעַל פְּנֵי הָאֲדָמָה

מֵאָדָם עַד־בְּהֵמָה

עַד־רֶמֶשׂ וְעַד־עוֹף הַשָּׁמָיִם

כִּי נִחַמְתִּי כִּי עֲשִׂיתִם:

8. וְנֹחַ

מָצָא חֵן בְּעֵינֵי יְהֹוָה:

After the Torah reading, recite the following blessing.

בָּרוּךְ אַתָּה יְיָ אֱלֹהֵינוּ מֶלֶךְ הָעוֹלָם, אֲשֶׁר נָתַן לָנוּ תּוֹרַת אֱמֶת,

וְחַיֵּי עוֹלָם נָטַע בְּתוֹכֵנוּ. בָּרוּךְ אַתָּה יְיָ, נוֹתֵן הַתּוֹרָה.

We praise You, Adonai our God, Ruler of the universe,
Who planted eternal life among us by giving us a Teaching of truth.

We praise You, Adonai, the Giver of Torah.

HAFTARAH IN ENGLISH: YISH'AYAH / ISAIAH 42: 5 TO 43: 10 (OR 42: 5-21)

What's the story so far?

The time of the Torah has long since passed. After a long exile in Mitzra'im (Egypt), the nation of Yisra'el returns to Cana'an and establishes a kingdom under the leadership of David and Shlomo (roughly 3000-ish years ago). Following Shlomo's death, a civil war breaks out that divides the kingdom into Yisra'el in the north and Yehudah in the south. The kingdoms coexist for 200 years until Yisra'el is conquered by Ashur (the Assyrian empire) in 722-720 BCE. Its people are deported and lost to history. Yehudah survives until Bavel (the Babylonian empire) conquers them and exiles the population (596-586 BCE).

Who's Yish'ayah and why does he have a book?

Yish'ayah was a prophet of God. A "prophet" was someone who had a special gift for communicating God's inspiring message to the people, leaders, and — quite often — kings of Yisra'el. Some prophets were employees of the king. Others were recognized as community leaders. Still others travelled from place to place spreading word of God's ethical requirements. Some are recorded as having performed miracles. The time of the prophets stretches from Moshe (3200-ish years ago) to Mal'ahi (2400-ish years ago). Regardless of who they were or when they lived, they all felt the same divine call to leave their professions and become God's social and moral conscience to the people.

The book of *Yish'ayah* is a compilation of at least two different prophets who lived roughly 200 years apart. Chapters one to thirty-nine belong to the first Yish'ayah who lived 2800-ish years ago during the time of the kings of Yisra'el. Chapters forty to sixty-six belong to the second Yish'ayah who lived during the Babylonian Exile, 2600-ish years ago.

THE HAFTARAH AND ITS BLESSINGS IN HEBREW

Before the Haftarah reading, recite one of the following blessings.
Your rabbi or teacher will tell you which one is appropriate for your community.

בָּרוּךְ אַתָּה יְיָ אֱלֹהֵינוּ מֶלֶךְ הָעוֹלָם,

אֲשֶׁר בָּחַר בִּנְבִיאִים טוֹבִים,

וְרָצָה בְדִבְרֵיהֶם הַנֶּאֱמָרִים בֶּאֱמֶת.

בָּרוּךְ אַתָּה יְיָ,

הַבּוֹחֵר בַּתּוֹרָה וּבְמֹשֶׁה עַבְדּוֹ,

וּבְיִשְׂרָאֵל עַמּוֹ,

וּבִנְבִיאֵי הָאֱמֶת וָצֶדֶק.

בָּרוּךְ אַתָּה יְיָ אֱלֹהֵינוּ מֶלֶךְ הָעוֹלָם,

אֲשֶׁר בָּחַר בִּנְבִיאִים טוֹבִים,

וְרָצָה בְדִבְרֵיהֶם הַנֶּאֱמָרִים בֶּאֱמֶת.

בָּרוּךְ אַתָּה יְיָ,

הַבּוֹחֵר בַּתּוֹרָה וּבְמֹשֶׁה עַבְדּוֹ,

וּבִנְבִיאֵי הָאֱמֶת וָצֶדֶק.

We praise You, Adonai our God,
Ruler of the universe,
Who appointed good prophets,
and Who expected lessons of truth
in the things they said.

We praise You, Adonai,
Who chose the Torah,
and Moshe, God's servant,
and Yisra'el, God's people,
and prophets of truth and righteousness.

We praise You, Adonai our God,
Ruler of the universe,
Who appointed good prophets,
and Who expected lessons of truth
in the things they said.

We praise You, Adonai,
Who chose the Torah,
and Moshe, God's servant,
and prophets of truth and righteousness.

What can I expect from this Haftarah?

This Haftarah is an excerpt from the second Yish'ayah who lived during the Babylonian Exile. He was one of a small group of community leaders who predicted the end of the Exile and a return to the land of Yisra'el. He also helped to reshape and reconstruct Yisra'el's culture, making it possible to remain Jewish without living in the Promised Land. Yish'ayah uses a lot of fancy and confusing metaphors. As you read them, keep Yish'ayah's priorities in mind: (1) he uses creative images to describe the relationship between God and the Jewish people; (2) he uses vivid symbols to describe God's actions in the world; and (3) he uses fancy language to explain why the Jews are in exile and how God wants to reconnect with them.

Without further ado, on to the Haftarah...

REASON FOR YISRA'EL'S PUNISHMENT

42: 5-12

These are the words of Adonai, the God who created and stretched out the heavens, the God who spread out the land and everything in it, the God who gives the breath of life to all who live on it, and the God who gives the spirit of life to all who walk on it:

I, Adonai, call to you in righteousness! I will hold your hand and I will watch over you. I will present you to the other nations as a people bound by My Brit — as a light to the other nations that opens the eyes of the blind, rescues prisoners, and saves those who sit in dark dungeons. I am Adonai! I will not surrender My glory to another. I will not surrender My praises to idols.

This Haftarah contrasts the themes of punishment and restoration. What are the connections between Yish'ayah's message to the exiles of Yisra'el and the story of Adam and Eve? What is the message about punishment and consequences from the parashah? How does the Haftarah modify this message?

Brit: The בְּרִית is the Agreement between Adonai and the people of Yisra'el. Adonai promises to provide wealth, land, healthy harvests, and security, and in exchange Yisra'el agrees to follow the Mitzvot. For two examples, see chapter 15 of *Bereshit / Genesis* and chapter 19 of *Shemot / Exodus*. Brit is usually translated as "Covenant".

Opens the eyes of the blind: Yish'ayah uses fancy imagery to make a point. He believes that the Babylonian Exile is God's punishment for Yisra'el's sins, and that if Yisra'el wants to be rescued they need to "see the light" and change their behavior. So whom is he referring to when he says "blind"? Who "sits in a dark dungeon"?

Chapter 42

5. כֹּה־אָמַ֞ר

הָאֵ֣ל ׀ יְהוָ֗ה

בּוֹרֵ֤א הַשָּׁמַ֙יִם֙ וְנ֣וֹטֵיהֶ֔ם

רֹקַ֥ע הָאָ֖רֶץ וְצֶאֱצָאֶ֑יהָ

נֹתֵ֤ן נְשָׁמָה֙ לָעָ֣ם עָלֶ֔יהָ

וְר֖וּחַ לַהֹלְכִ֥ים בָּֽהּ׃

6. אֲנִ֧י יְהוָ֛ה

קְרָאתִ֥יךָֽ בְצֶ֖דֶק וְאַחְזֵ֣ק בְּיָדֶ֑ךָ

וְאֶצָּרְךָ֗

וְאֶתֶּנְךָ֛

לִבְרִ֥ית עָ֖ם לְא֥וֹר גּוֹיִֽם׃

7. לִפְקֹ֖חַ עֵינַ֣יִם עִוְר֑וֹת

לְהוֹצִ֤יא מִמַּסְגֵּר֙ אַסִּ֔יר

מִבֵּ֥ית כֶּ֖לֶא יֹ֥שְׁבֵי חֹֽשֶׁךְ׃

8. אֲנִ֥י יְהוָ֖ה ה֣וּא שְׁמִ֑י

וּכְבוֹדִי֙ לְאַחֵ֣ר לֹֽא־אֶתֵּ֔ן

וּתְהִלָּתִ֖י לַפְּסִילִֽים׃

9. הָרִֽאשֹׁנ֖וֹת הִנֵּה־בָ֑אוּ

וַֽחֲדָשׁוֹת֙ אֲנִ֣י מַגִּ֔יד

בְּטֶ֥רֶם תִּצְמַ֖חְנָה אַשְׁמִ֥יע אֶתְכֶֽם׃

10. שִׁ֤ירוּ לַֽיהוָה֙ שִׁ֣יר חָדָ֔שׁ

תְּהִלָּת֖וֹ מִקְצֵ֣ה הָאָ֑רֶץ

יוֹרְדֵ֤י הַיָּם֙ וּמְלֹא֔וֹ

אִיִּ֖ים וְיֹשְׁבֵיהֶֽם׃

11. יִשְׂא֤וּ מִדְבָּר֙ וְעָרָ֔יו

חֲצֵרִ֖ים תֵּשֵׁ֣ב קֵדָ֑ר

יָרֹ֙נּוּ֙ יֹ֣שְׁבֵי סֶ֔לַע

מֵרֹ֥אשׁ הָרִ֖ים יִצְוָֽחוּ׃

12. יָשִׂ֥ימוּ לַֽיהוָ֖ה כָּב֑וֹד

וּתְהִלָּת֖וֹ בָּאִיִּ֥ים יַגִּֽידוּ׃

13. יְהוָה֙ כַּגִּבּ֣וֹר יֵצֵ֔א

כְּאִ֥ישׁ מִלְחָמ֖וֹת יָעִ֣יר קִנְאָ֑ה

יָרִ֙יעַ֙ אַף־יַצְרִ֔יחַ

עַל־אֹיְבָ֖יו יִתְגַּבָּֽר׃

Don't you see that what was predicted in the past came true? Now I make new predictions! I will describe them now before they happen. To the people down by the sea and out near the coastlands: sing to Adonai a new song of praise from all the ends of the earth! Let the wilderness and its cities cry out! The villages of Kedar and the people of Selah shout out, and from the mountain's peak they call. Let them give glory to Adonai, and sing God's praises on the coastland.

> 42:13-21
> Many synagogues end at verse 21.

Adonai advances like a hero and God's jealousy is roused like a warrior, roaring and charging at God's enemies.

For too long I have held my peace, keeping still and holding Myself back. Now I will shout like a woman in labor, gasping and panting! I will level mountains and hills and dry up their vegetation! I will turn rivers into islands

The darkness they see before them...: Remember that Yish'ayah is big on imagery. He's extending his blindness metaphor. How do you think God will turn their "darkness" into "light"? What sorts of people live in "darkness"? There's a hint at the end of the paragraph...

My servant...: Is Yish'ayah the "servant" and the "messenger"? Are the people of Yisra'el the "servant" and the "messenger"? Is there another possibility? Explore your ideas!

and dry up the marshlands! I will take the blind on a road they do not know, and lead them by unfamiliar paths. The darkness they see before them I will turn to light, and the rough paths they walk on I will level out. These things I will do! I will not leave them unfinished! Those who trust in idols and say to them, "You are our gods" will be sent back in shame!

You who are deaf, listen! And you who are blind, look up and see! Who is truly blind, if not My servant? Who is truly deaf, if not My messenger? Who is so blind as one chosen to serve Adonai? He sees much but does not speak his opinion.

For the sake of My servant's righteousness, I seek to make My Teaching great and glorious.

14. הֶחֱשֵׁ֙יתִי֙ מֵ֣עוֹלָ֔ם
אַחֲרִ֖ישׁ אֶתְאַפָּ֑ק
כַּיּוֹלֵדָ֣ה אֶפְעֶ֔ה
אֶשֹּׁ֥ם וְאֶשְׁאַ֖ף יָֽחַד׃

15. אַחֲרִ֤יב הָרִים֙ וּגְבָע֔וֹת
וְכָל־עֶשְׂבָּ֖ם אוֹבִ֑ישׁ
וְשַׂמְתִּ֤י נְהָרוֹת֙ לָֽאִיִּ֔ים
וַאֲגַמִּ֖ים אוֹבִֽישׁ׃

16. וְהוֹלַכְתִּ֣י עִוְרִ֗ים
בְּדֶ֙רֶךְ֙ לֹ֣א יָדָ֔עוּ
בִּנְתִיב֥וֹת לֹֽא־יָדְע֖וּ אַדְרִיכֵ֑ם
אָשִׂים֩ מַחְשָׁ֨ךְ לִפְנֵיהֶ֜ם לָא֗וֹר
וּמַֽעֲקַשִּׁים֙ לְמִישׁ֔וֹר
אֵ֚לֶּה הַדְּבָרִ֔ים
עֲשִׂיתִ֖ם וְלֹ֥א עֲזַבְתִּֽים׃

17. נָסֹ֤גוּ אָחוֹר֙ יֵבֹ֣שׁוּ בֹ֔שֶׁת
הַבֹּטְחִ֖ים בַּפָּ֑סֶל
הָאֹמְרִ֥ים לְמַסֵּכָ֖ה אַתֶּ֥ם אֱלֹהֵֽינוּ׃

18. הַחֵרְשִׁ֖ים שְׁמָ֑עוּ
וְהַעִוְרִ֖ים הַבִּ֥יטוּ לִרְאֽוֹת׃

19. מִ֤י עִוֵּר֙ כִּ֣י אִם־עַבְדִּ֔י
וְחֵרֵ֖שׁ כְּמַלְאָכִ֣י אֶשְׁלָ֑ח
מִ֤י עִוֵּר֙ כִּמְשֻׁלָּ֔ם
וְעִוֵּ֖ר כְּעֶ֥בֶד יְהוָֽה׃

20. רָאִ֥ית [רָא֛וֹת] רַבּ֖וֹת וְלֹ֣א תִשְׁמֹ֑ר
פָּק֥וֹחַ אָזְנַ֖יִם וְלֹ֥א יִשְׁמָֽע׃

21. יְהוָ֥ה חָפֵ֖ץ לְמַ֣עַן צִדְק֑וֹ
יַגְדִּ֥יל תּוֹרָ֖ה וְיַאְדִּֽיר׃

Many communities end here.

22. וְהוּא֮ עַם־בָּ֣זוּז וְשָׁסוּי֒
הָפֵ֤חַ בַּחוּרִים֙ כֻּלָּ֔ם
וּבְבָתֵּ֥י כְלָאִ֖ים הָחְבָּ֑אוּ
הָי֤וּ לָבַז֙ וְאֵ֣ין מַצִּ֔יל
מְשִׁסָּ֖ה וְאֵין־אֹמֵ֥ר הָשַֽׁב׃

33

42: 22-25

But this nation is ruined and spoiled! They're trapped in holes and locked in dungeons! They're hunted with no-one to rescue them, and they're stolen from with no-one to demand repayment. Who among you will do something about this? Who will listen and keep it in mind from now on? Who gave **Ya'akov** to

> **Ya'akov:** "Ya'akov" and "Yisra'el" both refer to the Jewish people. To find out why Yisra'el is often called "Ya'akov", look to the story of Ya'akov in the book of *Bereshit.* In particular, look up a famous wrestling match in chapter 32.
>
> **Him:** Meaning Ya'akov. Or Yisra'el. Or the people of Yisra'el. Or the ancient Jews. Take your pick — to Yish'ayah, they're all the same!

thieves and brought Yisra'el to ruin? It was Adonai, whom we sinned against! We didn't follow God's ways and we didn't listen to God's Teachings. So God poured fury, anger, and war upon **him**. It blazed around **him** but he didn't notice; it burned before him but he didn't take it to heart.

GOD WILL RESTORE YISRA'EL

43: 1-8

But now, these are the words of Adonai — the One who created you, O Ya'akov, and the One who made you, O Yisra'el:

Do not fear. I will save you. I will call you by name. You are Mine. I will be with you when you pass through water so the rivers do not drown you. When you walk through fire, you will not be burned, nor will the flame scorch you. For I am Adonai your God, the Holy One of Yisra'el, your Savior. I present Mitzra'im as your ransom — Kush and Seba instead of you. You are precious to me, you are honored, and I love you. So I will exchange men for you, and take nations in your place.

Do not fear, for I am with you. I will bring your descendants from the east and gather you together from the west. I will say to the north, "Give them to

> **I will exchange men for you…:** The Babylonian Exile is considered to be a kind of prison for the people of Yisra'el. The imagery here is like an exchange of prisoners. Yisra'el, who is now a prisoner, will be replaced in prison by their former captors (Mitzra'im).

me!" I will say to the south, "Do not hold them back! Bring my sons and my daughters from the ends of the earth — all who call My name, who I created and made for My glory!" I will free these people who are blind even though they have eyes, and deaf even though they have ears.

כִּי־תַעֲבֹר בַּמַּיִם אִתְּךָ־אָנִי 2.

וּבַנְּהָרוֹת לֹא יִשְׁטְפוּךָ

כִּי־תֵלֵךְ בְּמוֹ־אֵשׁ לֹא תִכָּוֶה

וְלֶהָבָה לֹא תִבְעַר־בָּךְ:

כִּי 3.

אֲנִי יהוה אֱלֹהֶיךָ

קְדוֹשׁ יִשְׂרָאֵל מוֹשִׁיעֶךָ

נָתַתִּי כָפְרְךָ מִצְרַיִם

כּוּשׁ וּסְבָא תַּחְתֶּיךָ:

מֵאֲשֶׁר יָקַרְתָּ בְעֵינַי 4.

נִכְבַּדְתָּ וַאֲנִי אֲהַבְתִּיךָ

וְאֶתֵּן אָדָם תַּחְתֶּיךָ

וּלְאֻמִּים תַּחַת נַפְשֶׁךָ:

אַל־תִּירָא כִּי־אִתְּךָ־אָנִי 5.

מִמִּזְרָח אָבִיא זַרְעֶךָ

וּמִמַּעֲרָב אֲקַבְּצֶךָּ:

מִי בָכֶם יַאֲזִין זֹאת 23.

יַקְשֵׁב וְיִשְׁמַע לְאָחוֹר:

מִי־נָתַן למשוסה [לִמְשִׁסָּה] יַעֲקֹב 24.

וְיִשְׂרָאֵל לְבֹזְזִים הֲלוֹא יהוה

זוּ חָטָאנוּ לוֹ

וְלֹא־אָבוּ בִדְרָכָיו הָלוֹךְ

וְלֹא שָׁמְעוּ בְּתוֹרָתוֹ:

וַיִּשְׁפֹּךְ עָלָיו חֵמָה אַפּוֹ 25.

וֶעֱזוּז מִלְחָמָה

וַתְּלַהֲטֵהוּ מִסָּבִיב וְלֹא יָדָע

וַתִּבְעַר־בּוֹ וְלֹא־יָשִׂים עַל־לֵב:

Chapter 43

וְעַתָּה 1.

כֹּה־אָמַר יהוה בֹּרַאֲךָ יַעֲקֹב

וְיֹצֶרְךָ יִשְׂרָאֵל

אַל־תִּירָא כִּי גְאַלְתִּיךָ

קָרָאתִי בְשִׁמְךָ לִי־אָתָּה:

43:9-10

Bring the nations together. Assemble the peoples! Which of them imagined this, or predicted events that came true? Let them bring witnesses to prove it so that others can hear them and declare, "It is the truth!"

You are my witnesses!

This is Adonai's message!

You are My servant whom I have chosen so that you will know Me and believe in Me, and understand that I am the One.

Before Me no god existed, nor will there be any after Me.

6. אֹמַר לַצָּפוֹן תֵּנִי

וּלְתֵימָן אַל־תִּכְלָאִי

הָבִיאִי בָנַי מֵרָחוֹק

וּבְנוֹתַי מִקְצֵה הָאָרֶץ:

7. כֹּל הַנִּקְרָא בִשְׁמִי

וְלִכְבוֹדִי בְּרָאתִיו

יְצַרְתִּיו אַף־עֲשִׂיתִיו:

8. הוֹצִיא עַם־עִוֵּר וְעֵינַיִם יֵשׁ

וְחֵרְשִׁים וְאָזְנַיִם לָמוֹ:

9. כָּל־הַגּוֹיִם

נִקְבְּצוּ יַחְדָּו

וְיֵאָסְפוּ לְאֻמִּים

מִי בָהֶם יַגִּיד זֹאת

וְרִאשֹׁנוֹת יַשְׁמִיעֻנוּ

יִתְּנוּ עֵדֵיהֶם וְיִצְדָּקוּ

וְיִשְׁמְעוּ וְיֹאמְרוּ אֱמֶת:

10. אַתֶּם עֵדַי נְאֻם־יְהוָֹה

וְעַבְדִּי אֲשֶׁר בָּחָרְתִּי

לְמַעַן תֵּדְעוּ

וְתַאֲמִינוּ לִי וְתָבִינוּ כִּי־אֲנִי הוּא

לְפָנַי לֹא־נוֹצַר אֵל

וְאַחֲרַי לֹא יִהְיֶה:

After the Haftarah reading, four blessings are recited. Note that there are choices for some of them. Your rabbi or teacher will tell you which ones are appropriate for your community.

(1)

בָּרוּךְ אַתָּה יְיָ אֱלֹהֵינוּ מֶלֶךְ הָעוֹלָם, צוּר כָּל הָעוֹלָמִים, צַדִּיק בְּכָל הַדּוֹרוֹת,

הָאֵל הַנֶּאֱמָן הָאוֹמֵר וְעֹשֶׂה, הַמְדַבֵּר וּמְקַיֵּם, שֶׁכָּל דְּבָרָיו אֱמֶת וָצֶדֶק.

נֶאֱמָן אַתָּה הוּא יְיָ אֱלֹהֵינוּ, וְנֶאֱמָנִים דְּבָרֶיךָ,

וְדָבָר אֶחָד מִדְּבָרֶיךָ אָחוֹר לֹא יָשׁוּב רֵיקָם, כִּי אֵל מֶלֶךְ נֶאֱמָן וְרַחֲמָן אָתָּה.

בָּרוּךְ אַתָּה יְיָ, הָאֵל הַנֶּאֱמָן בְּכָל דְּבָרָיו.

We praise You, Adonai our God, Ruler of the universe, Creator of all the worlds,
righteous in every generation. The faithful God Who does what God says,
Who speaks and fulfills it, Whose every word is true and just.

Adonai our God, You are faithful, Your words are faithful,
and nothing You say ever goes unfulfilled. You are a faithful and merciful God and Ruler.
We praise You, Adonai, the God who is faithful in every word.

(2)

רַחֵם עַל צִיּוֹן כִּי הִיא בֵּית חַיֵּינוּ,	רַחֵם עַל צִיּוֹן כִּי הִיא בֵּית חַיֵּינוּ,
וּלְעַמְּךָ יִשְׂרָאֵל תּוֹשִׁיעַ	וְלַעֲלוּבַת נֶפֶשׁ תּוֹשִׁיעַ
בִּמְהֵרָה בְיָמֵינוּ.	בִּמְהֵרָה בְיָמֵינוּ.
בָּרוּךְ אַתָּה יְיָ, מְשַׂמֵּחַ צִיּוֹן בְּבָנֶיהָ.	בָּרוּךְ אַתָּה יְיָ, מְשַׂמֵּחַ צִיּוֹן בְּבָנֶיהָ.

Show compassion for Tzion, for she is our lifelong home. Redeem Your people Israel soon and in our lifetime.

We praise You, Adonai, Who enables Tzion to rejoice with her children.

Show compassion for Tzion, for she is our lifelong home. Redeem her distressed spirit soon and in our lifetime.

We praise you, Adonai, Who enables Tzion to rejoice with her children.

3

שַׂמְּחֵנוּ, יְיָ אֱלֹהֵינוּ,

בְּאֵלִיָּהוּ הַנָּבִיא עַבְדֶּךָ,

וּבְמַלְכוּת בֵּית דָּוִד מְשִׁיחֶךָ.

בִּמְהֵרָה יָבֹא וְיָגֵל לִבֵּנוּ,

עַל כִּסְאוֹ לֹא יֵשֶׁב זָר,

וְלֹא יִנְחֲלוּ עוֹד אֲחֵרִים אֶת כְּבוֹדוֹ,

כִּי בְשֵׁם קָדְשְׁךָ נִשְׁבַּעְתָּ לּוֹ

שֶׁלֹּא יִכְבֶּה נֵרוֹ לְעוֹלָם וָעֶד.

בָּרוּךְ אַתָּה יְיָ, מָגֵן דָּוִד.

שַׂמְּחֵנוּ, יְיָ אֱלֹהֵינוּ,

בְּאֵלִיָּהוּ הַנָּבִיא עַבְדֶּךָ,

בִּמְהֵרָה יָבֹא וְיָגֵל לִבֵּנוּ.

וְהֵשִׁיב לֵב אָבוֹת עַל בָּנִים

וְלֵב בָּנִים עַל אֲבוֹתָם,

וּבֵיתְךָ בֵּית תְּפִילָה יִקָּרֵא לְכָל

הָעַמִּים.

בָּרוּךְ אַתָּה יְיָ, מֵבִיא שָׁלוֹם לָעַד.

Adonai our God,
grant us joy in Eliyahu Your prophet and
servant. Come soon to lift our hearts.
Turn the hearts of parents to their children,
and the hearts of children to their parents.
May Your House be called
a House of Prayer for all nations.
We praise You, Adonai,
Who brings peace for all time.

Adonai our God,
grant us joy in Eliyahu Your prophet
and servant, and in the reign of the dynasty
of David, Your anointed king.
May he come soon and lift our hearts.
Let no stranger sit on his throne.
Let others no longer inherit his glory,
for You swore to him by Your holy Name
that his light would never go out.
We praise You, Adonai,
Shield of David.

עַל הַתּוֹרָה, וְעַל הָעֲבוֹדָה, וְעַל הַנְּבִיאִים, וְעַל יוֹם הַשַּׁבָּת הַזֶּה,

שֶׁנָּתַתָּ לָנוּ, יְיָ אֱלֹהֵינוּ, לִקְדֻשָּׁה וְלִמְנוּחָה, לְכָבוֹד וּלְתִפְאָרֶת.

עַל הַכֹּל, יְיָ אֱלֹהֵינוּ, אֲנַחְנוּ מוֹדִים לָךְ, וּמְבָרְכִים אוֹתָךְ,

יִתְבָּרַךְ שִׁמְךָ בְּפִי כָל חַי תָּמִיד לְעוֹלָם וָעֶד.

בָּרוּךְ אַתָּה יְיָ, מְקַדֵּשׁ הַשַּׁבָּת.

For the Torah, for our worship, for the prophets, for today's Shabbat that
You, Adonai our God, gave us for holiness, rest, glory, and wonder:
for everything, Adonai our God, we thank You and praise You.
May the lips of every living thing glorify Your Name forever.

We praise You, Adonai, Who makes Shabbat holy.

SHABBAT MAHAR HODESH
(SHEMU'EL / SAMUEL 20: 18-42)

What's the story so far?

The time of Avraham, Sarah, Yitzhak, Rivkah, Ya'akov, Le'ah, Rahel, and their family has long since passed. After a long exile in Mitzra'im (Egypt), Moshe leads the nation of Yisra'el to Cana'an (Israel). Under the leadership of Yehoshu'a, they regain control over their ancient homeland and settle in tribal groups, but they cannot find peace. For more than a century, the tribes squabble among themselves. Finally, warfare with neighboring peoples forces the tribes of Yisra'el to unite under a king: Sha'ul (roughly 3000-ish years ago). Sha'ul soon buckles under the strain of uniting the tribes, listening to the prophet, Shmu'el, and jealously watching the rise of a brilliant young fighter named David. The books of *1 and 2 Shemu'el* describe the history of how the people of Yisra'el went from being a collection of tribes to a full-fledged kingdom.

Who's Shmu'el and why does he have a book?

Shmu'el was a prophet of God. A "prophet" is someone who has a special gift for communicating God's inspiring message to the people and leaders of Yisra'el. Before there was a kingdom, Yisra'el was organized into tribes. These tribes often squabbled, but they sometimes came together under the leadership of a charismatic chieftain called a "shofet". Shmu'el was the last of these shoftim (he was a shofet **and** a prophet. The adventures of the judges who lived before Shmu'el are recorded in the book of *Shoftim*.) The book of *Shmu'el* follows the lives of Shmu'el and the first two kings of Yisra'el: Sha'ul and David. Sha'ul was unable to unite the tribes of Yisra'el for very long, and he died in battle against the Pelishtim (Philistines). His famous general, David, became king after him. David was wildly successful, uniting the tribes and expanding the borders of Yisra'el to include most of the neighboring peoples. David established Jerusalem as the eternal capital of the nation of Yisra'el (3000-ish years ago) and he established his family as the ruling dynasty.

THE HAFTARAH AND ITS BLESSINGS

Before the Haftarah reading, recite one of these blessings.
Your rabbi or teacher will tell you which one is appropriate for your community.

בָּרוּךְ אַתָּה יְיָ אֱלֹהֵינוּ מֶלֶךְ הָעוֹלָם,

אֲשֶׁר בָּחַר בִּנְבִיאִים טוֹבִים,

וְרָצָה בְדִבְרֵיהֶם הַנֶּאֱמָרִים בֶּאֱמֶת.

בָּרוּךְ אַתָּה יְיָ,

הַבּוֹחֵר בַּתּוֹרָה וּבְמֹשֶׁה עַבְדּוֹ,

וּבְיִשְׂרָאֵל עַמּוֹ,

וּבִנְבִיאֵי הָאֱמֶת וָצֶדֶק.

We praise You, Adonai our God,
Ruler of the universe,
Who appointed good prophets,
and Who expected lessons of truth
in the things they said.

We praise You, Adonai,
Who chose the Torah,
and Moshe, God's servant,
and Yisra'el, God's people,
and prophets of truth and righteousness.

בָּרוּךְ אַתָּה יְיָ אֱלֹהֵינוּ מֶלֶךְ הָעוֹלָם,

אֲשֶׁר בָּחַר בִּנְבִיאִים טוֹבִים,

וְרָצָה בְדִבְרֵיהֶם הַנֶּאֱמָרִים בֶּאֱמֶת.

בָּרוּךְ אַתָּה יְיָ,

הַבּוֹחֵר בַּתּוֹרָה וּבְמֹשֶׁה עַבְדּוֹ,

וּבִנְבִיאֵי הָאֱמֶת וָצֶדֶק.

We praise You, Adonai our God,
Ruler of the universe,
Who appointed good prophets,
and Who expected lessons of truth
in the things they said.

We praise You, Adonai,
Who chose the Torah,
and Moshe, God's servant,
and prophets of truth and righteousness.

43

What can I expect from this Haftarah?

This Haftarah takes place in the middle of an action-packed story. King Sha'ul has become convinced that his famous general, David, wants to take over the throne. Sha'ul decides that the only way to protect the throne for his children is to kill David. But there's a problem: Sha'ul's oldest son, Yonatan, is best friends with David. By the time this Haftarah begins, Sha'ul has already tried to kill David, and Yonatan doesn't believe David when David tells him that Sha'ul wants him dead.

What's the connection to Rosh <u>H</u>odesh?

Rosh <u>H</u>odesh is a minor festival that marks the start of each new month. Sometimes it falls right after Shabbat ends. When this happens, *Shemu'el* 20: 18-42 replaces the regular Shabbat morning Haftarah. Why did our sages choose to do this? Keep reading and see if you can spot the connection(s) between the story of David / Yonatan / Sha'ul and Rosh <u>H</u>odesh.

And so, without further ado, on to the Haftarah...

18. וַיֹּאמֶר־לוֹ יְהוֹנָתָן מָחָר חֹדֶשׁ
וְנִפְקַדְתָּ
כִּי יִפָּקֵד מוֹשָׁבֶךָ:

19. וְשִׁלַּשְׁתָּ תֵּרֵד מְאֹד
וּבָאתָ אֶל־הַמָּקוֹם
אֲשֶׁר־נִסְתַּרְתָּ שָּׁם בְּיוֹם הַמַּעֲשֶׂה
וְיָשַׁבְתָּ
אֵצֶל הָאֶבֶן הָאָזֶל:

20. וַאֲנִי
שְׁלֹשֶׁת הַחִצִּים צִדָּה אוֹרֶה
לְשַׁלַּח־לִי לְמַטָּרָה:

21. וְהִנֵּה אֶשְׁלַח אֶת־הַנַּעַר
לֵךְ מְצָא אֶת־הַחִצִּים
אִם־אָמֹר אֹמַר לַנַּעַר
הִנֵּה הַחִצִּים מִמְּךָ ׀ וָהֵנָּה
קָחֶנּוּ ׀ וָבֹאָה כִּי־שָׁלוֹם לְךָ
וְאֵין דָּבָר חַי־יְהוָה:

22. וְאִם־כֹּה אֹמַר לָעֶלֶם
הִנֵּה הַחִצִּים מִמְּךָ וָהָלְאָה
לֵךְ
כִּי שִׁלַּחֲךָ יְהוָה:

23. וְהַדָּבָר
אֲשֶׁר דִּבַּרְנוּ אֲנִי וָאָתָּה
הִנֵּה יְהוָה
בֵּינִי וּבֵינְךָ עַד־עוֹלָם:

24. וַיִּסָּתֵר דָּוִד בַּשָּׂדֶה
וַיְהִי הַחֹדֶשׁ
וַיֵּשֶׁב הַמֶּלֶךְ
עַל [אֶל]־הַלֶּחֶם לֶאֱכוֹל:

25. וַיֵּשֶׁב הַמֶּלֶךְ עַל־מוֹשָׁבוֹ
כְּפַעַם ׀ בְּפַעַם
אֶל־מוֹשַׁב הַקִּיר
וַיָּקָם יְהוֹנָתָן
וַיֵּשֶׁב אַבְנֵר מִצַּד שָׁאוּל
וַיִּפָּקֵד מְקוֹם דָּוִד:

HATCHING THE SCHEME

20: 18-22

"The New Month festival is tomorrow," said Yonatan to David. "If your seat at my father's table remains empty, your absence will be noticed. So here's what we'll do: you hide in the countryside in the same place you hid before, by the stone of Azel. Three days from now, I'll go there and shoot three arrows off to the side of the stone, as if I was doing some target practice. I'll order my squire to collect the arrows. If I call to him, 'Hey — the arrows are on this side of you!' it will mean that things are fine for you at the king's court and you can come back. But if I call to my squire, 'Hey — the arrows are further away!' it will mean that you have to leave, that Adonai is sending you away."

20: 23-24

David liked the plan, but Yonatan continued. "But **regarding the arrangement you and I agreed to earlier** — Adonai is witness to the eternal bond between us."

David agreed and hid in the field, waiting for Yonatan's return.

Regarding the arrangement...: Yonatan is referring to the first part of their conversation that takes place right before the Haftarah. Yonatan has a feeling that David, not Yonatan, will be the next king even though David has made no attempt to seize the throne. So he and David agree that no matter what happens, there will be a permanent alliance between David's dynasty and Yonatan's. David will remain faithful to Yonatan and protect Yonatan's family even after Yonatan's death. Is this foreshadowing? Perhaps...

26. וְלֹא־דִבֶּר שָׁאוּל

מְאוּמָה בַּיּוֹם הַהוּא

כִּי אָמַר מִקְרֶה הוּא

בִּלְתִּי טָהוֹר

הוּא כִּי־לֹא טָהוֹר:

27. וַיְהִי מִמָּחֳרַת הַחֹדֶשׁ הַשֵּׁנִי

וַיִּפָּקֵד מְקוֹם דָּוִד

וַיֹּאמֶר שָׁאוּל אֶל־יְהוֹנָתָן בְּנוֹ

מַדּוּעַ

לֹא־בָא בֶן־יִשַׁי

גַם־תְּמוֹל גַם־הַיּוֹם אֶל־הַלָּחֶם:

28. וַיַּעַן יְהוֹנָתָן אֶת־שָׁאוּל

נִשְׁאֹל נִשְׁאַל דָּוִד

מֵעִמָּדִי עַד־בֵּית לָחֶם:

29. וַיֹּאמֶר

שַׁלְּחֵנִי נָא

כִּי זֶבַח מִשְׁפָּחָה לָנוּ בָּעִיר

וְהוּא צִוָּה־לִי אָחִי

וְעַתָּה

אִם־מָצָאתִי חֵן בְּעֵינֶיךָ

אִמָּלְטָה נָּא וְאֶרְאֶה אֶת־אֶחָי

עַל־כֵּן לֹא־בָא

אֶל־שֻׁלְחַן הַמֶּלֶךְ:

30. וַיִּחַר־אַף שָׁאוּל בִּיהוֹנָתָן

וַיֹּאמֶר לוֹ

בֶּן־נַעֲוַת הַמַּרְדּוּת

הֲלוֹא יָדַעְתִּי

כִּי־בֹחֵר אַתָּה לְבֶן־יִשַׁי

לְבָשְׁתְּךָ

וּלְבֹשֶׁת עֶרְוַת אִמֶּךָ:

47

RAGE AND SORROW

20: 25-29

When the celebration for the New Month came, King Sha'ul sat down to eat at the feast. He sat at the head of the table by the wall, as usual. Yonatan rose from his seat as **Avner** sat down at Sha'ul's side, but David's place was empty. Sha'ul didn't say anything about it. *Something's happened to David*, the king thought. *He must not have been able to cleanse himself in time for the New Month.*

However, when David's place was still empty the day after the New Month, Sha'ul turned to Yonatan. "Why hasn't the **son of Yishai** come to my table — not yesterday and not today?" he demanded.

> **Avner:** commander of Sha'ul's army.
>
> **Son of Yishai:** Yishai was David's father.

"He begged me for permission to go to Beit-Lehem," replied Yonatan. "He said to me, 'My family is sponsoring the sacrifice for our town and my brother demands my presence. Please, if you've found me worthy of you, grant me leave to see my family.' This is why he hasn't come to the king's table."

20: 30-34

Sha'ul became infuriated with his son. "You degenerate, mutinous child!" he roared. "You think I don't know that you've sided with the son of Yishai?! You shame yourself and your mother's whoring! You and your throne will ever be secure as long as the son of Yishai lives! Now bring him here so he can die!"

"Why should he die?" defied Yonatan. "What has he done?"

Flying into a rage, Sha'ul hurled his spear at his son, and Yonatan realized that his father truly meant to kill David. Yonatan left the table seething in anger. Out of grief for David and humiliation from his father, he ate nothing for the entire second day of the month.

> **Sha'ul became infuriated...:** At first glance, this looks like a major overreaction on Sha'ul's part. But set aside the details for a moment and ask yourself: does Sha'ul have legitimate concern? David wasn't just Yonatan's best friend; he was also married to Yonatan's sister, Mihal (a.k.a. Sha'ul's daughter.) Discuss your ideas.
>
> And what about Yonatan, caught between his best friend and his father? How might he be feeling? If he chooses one, he risks losing the other. What about Mihal, who doesn't appear in the Haftarah? Seeing the story through the eyes of different people is a great way to add dimension to the text. Talk to your teacher / rabbi about it!

31. כִּי כָל־הַיָּמִ֗ים

אֲשֶׁ֨ר בֶּן־יִשַׁי֙ חַי֙ עַל־הָ֣אֲדָמָ֔ה

לֹ֥א תִכּ֖וֹן אַתָּ֣ה וּמַלְכוּתֶ֑ךָ

וְעַתָּ֗ה

שְׁלַ֨ח וְקַ֤ח אֹתוֹ֙ אֵלַ֔י

כִּ֥י בֶן־מָ֖וֶת הֽוּא:

32. וַיַּ֨עַן֙ יְה֣וֹנָתָ֔ן

אֶת־שָׁא֖וּל אָבִ֑יו

וַיֹּ֥אמֶר אֵלָ֖יו

לָ֥מָּה יוּמַ֖ת מֶ֥ה עָשָֽׂה:

33. וַיָּ֧טֶל שָׁא֛וּל אֶת־הַחֲנִ֖ית

עָלָ֑יו לְהַכֹּת֑וֹ

וַיֵּ֨דַע֙ יְה֣וֹנָתָ֔ן

כִּֽי־כָ֥לָה הִ֛יא

מֵעִ֥ם אָבִ֖יו לְהָמִ֥ית אֶת־דָּוִֽד:

34. וַיָּ֥קָם יְהוֹנָתָ֖ן

מֵעִ֥ם הַשֻּׁלְחָ֖ן בָּחֳרִי־אָ֑ף

וְלֹא־אָכַ֜ל

בְּיוֹם־הַחֹ֤דֶשׁ הַשֵּׁנִי֙ לֶ֔חֶם

כִּ֤י נֶעְצַב֙ אֶל־דָּוִ֔ד

כִּ֥י הִכְלִמ֖וֹ אָבִֽיו:

35. וַיְהִ֣י בַבֹּ֔קֶר

וַיֵּצֵ֧א יְהוֹנָתָ֛ן

הַשָּׂדֶ֖ה לְמוֹעֵ֣ד דָּוִ֑ד

וְנַ֥עַר קָטֹ֖ן עִמּֽוֹ:

36. וַיֹּ֣אמֶר לְנַעֲר֔וֹ

רֻ֗ץ

מְצָ֥א נָא֙ אֶת־הַ֣חִצִּ֔ים

אֲשֶׁ֥ר אָנֹכִ֖י מוֹרֶ֑ה

הַנַּ֣עַר רָ֔ץ

וְהֽוּא־יָרָ֥ה הַחֵ֖צִי לְהַעֲבִרֽוֹ:

20:35-42

The following morning, Yonatan went out to the field with his squire at the time he and David had agreed to. "Go and fetch the arrows I shoot," he told the boy.

The squire ran off as Yonatan shot arrows past him. When the boy reached the spot where the arrows landed, Yonatan shouted, "Hey — the arrows are further away! Hurry, as fast as you can! Don't linger here!"

The squire gathered up the arrows and returned to his lord. He suspected nothing; only Yonatan and David knew the plan. Handing his weapons to the squire, Yonatan instructed, "Bring these back to the city."

As soon as the boy was gone, David stood up from the spot to the south where he was hiding. He fell to the ground and bowed low three times. They kissed each other farewell and wept together, though David's anguish was greater.

"Go in peace," sobbed Yonatan. "We've sworn in Adonai's Name that Adonai is a witness between you and me, and between my offspring and yours, forever."

> Why do you think the Rabbanim of old chose this particular passage as the Haftarah for *Mahar Hodesh?* Your teacher / rabbi can help you explore the themes embedded in this Haftarah that might help us as we start fresh in a new month.

37. וַיָּבֹא הַנַּעַר עַד־מְקוֹם הַחֵצִי
אֲשֶׁר יָרָה יְהוֹנָתָן
וַיִּקְרָא יְהוֹנָתָן
אַחֲרֵי הַנַּעַר וַיֹּאמֶר
הֲלוֹא הַחֵצִי מִמְּךָ וָהָלְאָה:

38. וַיִּקְרָא יְהוֹנָתָן אַחֲרֵי הַנַּעַר
מְהֵרָה חוּשָׁה אַל־תַּעֲמֹד
וַיְלַקֵּט
נַעַר יְהוֹנָתָן אֶת־הַחֵצִי [הַחִצִּים]
וַיָּבֹא אֶל־אֲדֹנָיו:

39. וְהַנַּעַר לֹא־יָדַע מְאוּמָה
אַךְ יְהוֹנָתָן וְדָוִד
יָדְעוּ אֶת־הַדָּבָר:

40. וַיִּתֵּן יְהוֹנָתָן אֶת־כֵּלָיו
אֶל־הַנַּעַר אֲשֶׁר־לוֹ
וַיֹּאמֶר לוֹ
לֵךְ הָבֵיא הָעִיר:

41. הַנַּעַר בָּא
וְדָוִד
קָם מֵאֵצֶל הַנֶּגֶב
וַיִּפֹּל לְאַפָּיו אַרְצָה
וַיִּשְׁתַּחוּ שָׁלֹשׁ פְּעָמִים
וַיִּשְׁקוּ | אִישׁ אֶת־רֵעֵהוּ
וַיִּבְכּוּ אִישׁ אֶת־רֵעֵהוּ
עַד־דָּוִד הִגְדִּיל:

42. וַיֹּאמֶר יְהוֹנָתָן
לְדָוִד לֵךְ לְשָׁלוֹם
אֲשֶׁר נִשְׁבַּעְנוּ שְׁנֵינוּ אֲנַחְנוּ
בְּשֵׁם יְהוָה לֵאמֹר
יְהוָה
יִהְיֶה | בֵּינִי וּבֵינֶךָ
וּבֵין זַרְעִי
וּבֵין זַרְעֲךָ עַד־עוֹלָם:

CLOSING BLESSINGS

After the Haftarah reading, four blessings are recited. Note that there are choices for some of them. Your rabbi or teacher will tell you which ones are appropriate for your community.

① (1)

בָּרוּךְ אַתָּה יְיָ אֱלֹהֵינוּ מֶלֶךְ הָעוֹלָם, צוּר כָּל הָעוֹלָמִים, צַדִּיק בְּכָל הַדּוֹרוֹת,

הָאֵל הַנֶּאֱמָן הָאוֹמֵר וְעוֹשֶׂה, הַמְדַבֵּר וּמְקַיֵּם, שֶׁכָּל דְּבָרָיו אֱמֶת וָצֶדֶק.

נֶאֱמָן אַתָּה הוּא יְיָ אֱלֹהֵינוּ, וְנֶאֱמָנִים דְּבָרֶיךָ,

וְדָבָר אֶחָד מִדְּבָרֶיךָ אָחוֹר לֹא יָשׁוּב רֵיקָם, כִּי אֵל מֶלֶךְ נֶאֱמָן וְרַחֲמָן אָתָּה.

בָּרוּךְ אַתָּה יְיָ, הָאֵל הַנֶּאֱמָן בְּכָל דְּבָרָיו.

We praise You, Adonai our God, Ruler of the universe, Creator of all the worlds, righteous in every generation. The faithful God Who does what God says, Who speaks and fulfills it, Whose every word is true and just.

Adonai our God, You are faithful, Your words are faithful, and nothing You say ever goes unfulfilled. You are a faithful and merciful God and Ruler. We praise You, Adonai, the God who is faithful in every word.

② (2)

רַחֵם עַל צִיּוֹן כִּי הִיא בֵּית חַיֵּינוּ,	רַחֵם עַל צִיּוֹן כִּי הִיא בֵּית חַיֵּינוּ,
וּלְעַמְּךָ יִשְׂרָאֵל תּוֹשִׁיעַ	וְלַעֲלוּבַת נֶפֶשׁ תּוֹשִׁיעַ
בִּמְהֵרָה בְיָמֵינוּ.	בִּמְהֵרָה בְיָמֵינוּ.
בָּרוּךְ אַתָּה יְיָ, מְשַׂמֵּחַ צִיּוֹן בְּבָנֶיהָ.	בָּרוּךְ אַתָּה יְיָ, מְשַׂמֵּחַ צִיּוֹן בְּבָנֶיהָ.

Show compassion for Tzion, for she is our lifelong home. Redeem Your people Israel soon and in our lifetime.

We praise You, Adonai, Who enables Tzion to rejoice with her children.

Show compassion for Tzion, for she is our lifelong home. Redeem her distressed spirit soon and in our lifetime.

We praise you, Adonai, Who enables Tzion to rejoice with her children.

3

שַׂמְּחֵנוּ, יְיָ אֱלֹהֵינוּ,

בְּאֵלִיָּהוּ הַנָּבִיא עַבְדֶּךָ,

וּבְמַלְכוּת בֵּית דָּוִד מְשִׁיחֶךָ.

בִּמְהֵרָה יָבֹא וְיָגֵל לִבֵּנוּ,

עַל כִּסְאוֹ לֹא יֵשֶׁב זָר,

וְלֹא יִנְחֲלוּ עוֹד אֲחֵרִים אֶת כְּבוֹדוֹ,

כִּי בְשֵׁם קָדְשְׁךָ נִשְׁבַּעְתָּ לוֹ

שֶׁלֹּא יִכְבֶּה נֵרוֹ לְעוֹלָם וָעֶד.

בָּרוּךְ אַתָּה יְיָ, מָגֵן דָּוִד.

Adonai our God,
grant us joy in Eliyahu Your prophet
and servant, and in the reign of the dynasty
of David, Your anointed king.
May he come soon and lift our hearts.
Let no stranger sit on his throne.
Let others no longer inherit his glory,
for You swore to him by Your holy Name
that his light would never go out.
We praise You, Adonai,
Shield of David.

שַׂמְּחֵנוּ, יְיָ אֱלֹהֵינוּ,

בְּאֵלִיָּהוּ הַנָּבִיא עַבְדָּךְ,

בִּמְהֵרָה יָבֹא וְיָגֵל לִבֵּנוּ.

וְהָשֵׁיב לֵב אָבוֹת עַל בָּנִים

וְלֵב בָּנִים עַל אֲבוֹתָם,

וּבֵיתְךָ בֵּית תְּפִילָּה יִקָּרֵא לְכָל הָעַמִּים.

בָּרוּךְ אַתָּה יְיָ, מֵבִיא שָׁלוֹם לָעַד.

Adonai our God,
grant us joy in Eliyahu Your prophet and
servant. Come soon to lift our hearts.
Turn the hearts of parents to their children,
and the hearts of children to their parents.
May Your House be called
a House of Prayer for all nations.
We praise You, Adonai,
Who brings peace for all time.

THE CLOSING BLESSINGS CONTINUE ON THE NEXT PAGE.

④

עַל הַתּוֹרָה, וְעַל הָעֲבוֹדָה, וְעַל הַנְּבִיאִים, וְעַל יוֹם הַשַּׁבָּת הַזֶּה,

שֶׁנָּתַתָּ לָּנוּ, יְיָ אֱלֹהֵינוּ, לִקְדֻשָּׁה וְלִמְנוּחָה, לְכָבוֹד וּלְתִפְאֶרֶת.

עַל הַכֹּל, יְיָ אֱלֹהֵינוּ, אֲנַחְנוּ מוֹדִים לָךְ, וּמְבָרְכִים אוֹתָךְ,

יִתְבָּרַךְ שִׁמְךָ בְּפִי כָּל חַי תָּמִיד לְעוֹלָם וָעֶד.

בָּרוּךְ אַתָּה יְיָ, מְקַדֵּשׁ הַשַּׁבָּת.

For the Torah, for our worship, for the prophets, for today's Shabbat that
You, Adonai our God, gave us for holiness, rest, glory, and wonder:
for everything, Adonai our God, we thank You and praise You.
May the lips of every living thing glorify Your Name forever.

We praise You, Adonai, Who makes Shabbat holy.

TA'AMEI HA-MIKRA: TROP CHARTS

Let's face it: learning trop can be very difficult. Most of us are used to the idea that each musical sign represents a single tone, but with trop, most signs (*ta'amim*) represent musical phrases. To add to the difficulty, there are 28 separate trop signs — each with a unique musical phrase, and sometimes the phrasing changes depending on the combination of *ta'amim* (though very few readings contain all 28 *ta'amim*). Sure, you can find sheet music to help you out, but if you're like me and don't read music, you might wind up more confused. Oy!

I developed the charts in this section to help people like me. Most of the *ta'amim* are grouped into sequences that are used commonly in the Tana<u>h</u>. The grids enable the teacher and the student to chart the music as it goes higher or lower.

These charts have proven quite helpful with my own students. I hope you find them just as useful!

אֶתְנַחְתָּא

Etna<u>h</u>ta divides a verse into two broad ideas. Tipha, Zakef, Segol, and Shalshelet then divide Etna<u>h</u>ta into smaller ideas. Etna<u>h</u>ta always comes after Tiphah.

Common Patterns

מֵירְכָא טִפְחָא מוּנַח אֶתְנַחְתָּא

טִפְחָא מוּנַח אֶתְנַחְתָּא

מֵירְכָא טִפְחָא אֶתְנַחְתָּא

טִפְחָא אֶתְנַחְתָּא

מוּנַח מוּנַח אֶתְנַחְתָּא

What's the point of all this trop?

Apart from musical notations, the trop (or, more properly, *te'amim*) tell us where to put the correct emphasis in each word and sentence. They also function as grammatical and syntactical notations, telling us when to pause in our reading, when to read quickly, etc. So we don't just read the punctuation — we sing it! There are seven distinct vocal systems for chanting the Tana<u>h</u>. Most people are familiar with Torah and Haftarah. See if you can find out what the other five are!

TORAH TROP

Top section

סוֹף־פָּסוּק

Sof Pasuk is also called סִלּוּק (Siluk). It marks the end of a verse. Tipha and Zakef subdivide Sof Pasuk into smaller ideas. Sof Pasuk always comes after Tiphah.

Common Patterns

פָּסוּק סוֹף־פָּסוּק

זָקֵף סוֹף־פָּסוּק

זָקֵף טִפְחָא סוֹף־פָּסוּק

טִפְחָא סוֹף־פָּסוּק

מֵרְכָא טִפְחָא סוֹף־פָּסוּק

מֵרְכָא טִפְחָא זָקֵף סוֹף־פָּסוּק

Bottom section

אֶתְנַחְתָּא

Etnahta divides a verse into two broad ideas. Tipha, Zakef, Segol, and Shalshelet then divide Etnahta into smaller ideas. Etnahta always comes after Tiphah.

Common Patterns

אֶתְנַחְתָּא

טִפְחָא אֶתְנַחְתָּא

זָקֵף טִפְחָא אֶתְנַחְתָּא

מֵרְכָא טִפְחָא אֶתְנַחְתָּא

טִפְחָא מֵרְכָא זָקֵף טִפְחָא אֶתְנַחְתָּא

Common Patterns

זָקֵף גָּדוֹל

זָקֵף קָטוֹן אֶתְנַחְתָּ֑א טִפְחָ֖א

זָקֵף אַשְׁפָּ֔א

זָקֵף קָ֔טֹן
(see Yetiv card)

זָקֵף קָטוֹן קָ֔טֹן
(see Yetiv card)

זָקֵף–גָּדוֹל

Zakef divides Etnaḥta and Sof Pasuk into smaller ideas, but only if they already have a Tipḥa. Reviʾa, Pashta and Yetiv suubdivide Zakef into even simpler ideas. Zakef-Katon (a.k.a Katon) is more common than Zakef-Gadol.

Common Patterns

דַּרְגָ֧א תְּבִ֛יר טִפְחָ֖א

זַרְקָ֮א סֶגּוֹל֮ תְּבִ֛יר

מֵרְכָ֥א תְּבִ֛יר טִפְחָ֖א

מַהְפַּ֤ךְ פַּשְׁטָא֙ תְּבִ֛יר

דַּרְגָ֧א תְּבִ֛יר אַזְלָ֤א

תְּבִיר

When a Tipḥa idea has three or more words, it needs to be subdivided. We use Tevir for this subdivision.

57

TORAH TROP

Common Patterns

זָקֵף-קָטֹן

Common Patterns

סֶגּוֹל אֵלֶּה
סֶגוֹל זָרְקָא מֻנַּח סֶגוֹל
סֶגוֹל מֻנַּח

רְבִיעִי

Common Patterns

When Tipḥa, Zakef, or Segol need to be subdivided and they have one or two Tevirs, Revi'a is used as the Divider.

גֶּרֶשׁ

Common Patterns

If a Tevir, Pashta, Revi'a or Zarka needs to be subdivided, the subdivider is usually Geresh or Gershayim.

TORAH TROP

Common Patterns

פַּשְׁטָ֙א

> **פַּשְׁטָ֙א**
>
> Pashta is only used on the last or second-last syllable of a word. If a Pashta is needed on the first syllable, we use Yetiv, instead. Yetiv never uses a Link.

Common Patterns

גֵּרְשַׁ֞יִם

> **גֵּרְשַׁ֞יִם**
>
> If a Tevir, Pashta, Revi'a or Zarka needs to be subdivided, the subdivider is usually Geresh or Gershayim.

Common Patterns

מְנוּחָה פָּזֵר

									בַּיּ הַּ רֹ		
									בֵּ		
									הַ יֹ		

פָּזֵר

Pazer is used to subdivide Tevir, Revi'a, Pashta, and Zarka. Pazer can be linked to up to six Munahs.

Common Patterns

מְנוּחָה הַתְּלִישָׁה־גְדוֹלָה

									בַּיּ הַּ רֹ		
									הֹּ הֹּ		
									אָ לִ		

הַתְּלִישָׁה־גְדוֹלָה

When Tevir, Revi'a, Pashta, or Zarka need to be subdivided, Telishah-Gedolah is sometimes used. When the accent is not on the first syllable, a second Telishah-Gedolah is often added to mark the stress. Telishah-Gedolah can be linked to up to six Munahs.

HAFTARAH TROP

Top section

Common Patterns

מִפְּטֶף אָרְיָא סוֹף־פָּסוּק
מִרְכָּא טִפְּחָא סוֹף־פָּסוּק
מִרְכָּא טִפְּחָא מִרְכָּא סוֹף־פָּסוּק
מֵרְכָּא טִפְּחָא מֵרְכָּא סוֹף־פָּסוּק
טִפְּחָא מֵרְכָּא סוֹף־פָּסוּק

סוֹף־פָּסוּק

Sof Pasuk is also called סִלּוּק (Siluk). It marks the end of a verse. Tipha and Zakef subdivide Sof Pasuk into smaller ideas. Sof Pasuk always comes after Tiphah.

וַיְהִי אֶת אֲשֶׁר אֹתוֹ וַיְהִי אֵת אֲשֶׁר חוּם הֵ דֶר וַיְהִי

Bottom section

Common Patterns

אֶתְנַחְתָּא מֵרְכָּא טִפְּחָא מֵרְכָּא
אֶתְנַחְתָּא מֵרְכָּא טִפְּחָא
אֶתְנַחְתָּא מֵרְכָּא טִפְּחָא מֵרְכָּא
אֶתְנַחְתָּא מֵרְכָּא טִפְּחָא
הֵ טִפְּחָא אֶתְנַחְתָּא

אֶתְנַחְתָּא

Etnahta divides a verse into two broad ideas. Tipha, Zakef, Segol, and Shalshelet then divide Etnahta into smaller ideas. Etnahta always comes after Tiphah.

וַיְהִי אֶת אֲשֶׁר אֹתוֹ וַהֵ דֶר אֵת אֲשֶׁר אֵת

HAFTARAH TROP

זָקֵף-קָטוֹן

Zakef divides Etnaḥta and Sof Pasuk into smaller ideas, but only if they already have a Tipha. Revi'a, Pashta and Yetiv suubdivide Zakef into even simpler ideas. Zakef-Katon (a.k.a Katon) is more common than Zakef-Gadol.

Common Patterns

מַהְפַּךְ פַּשְׁטָא זָקֵף קָטוֹן

מֻנַּח זָקֵף קָטוֹן

דַּרְגָּא תְּבִיר מַהְפַּךְ פַּשְׁטָא זָקֵף קָטוֹן

מַהְפַּךְ פַּשְׁטָא זָקֵף קָטוֹן

מֻנַּח זָקֵף קָטוֹן
(see Yetiv card)

זָקֵף קָטוֹן מֻנַּח זָקֵף קָטוֹן
(see Yetiv card)

טִפְּחָא

When a Tipha idea has three or more words, it needs to be subdivided. We use Tevir for this subdivision.

Common Patterns

מַהְפַּךְ פַּשְׁטָא מֻנַּח טִפְּחָא

מֵרְכָא טִפְּחָא

מֻנַּח מֵרְכָא טִפְּחָא

דַּרְגָּא תְּבִיר מֵרְכָא טִפְּחָא

דַּרְגָּא תְּבִיר טִפְּחָא

HAFTARAH TROP

Common Patterns

זָקֵף־גָּדוֹל

זָקֵף־גָּדוֹל

Zakef divides Etnahta and Sof Pasuk into smaller ideas, but only if they already have a Tipha, Revi'a, Pashta and Yetiv suubdivide Zakef into even simpler ideas. Zakef-Gadol is only found on short words and it never uses a Link.

Common Patterns

סֶגּוֹל מֻנַּח
סֶגּוֹל מֻנַּח זַרְקָא מֻנַּח
סֶגּוֹל אַזְלָא

סֶגּוֹל

Segol divides Etnahta into smaller ideas, but only if it already has a Tipha and at least one Zakef. Revi'a, Pashta, Yetiv, and Zarka subdivide Segol into simpler ideas. Segol never appears on the first word of a verse.

64

HAFTARAH TROP

Common Patterns

רְבִיעַ

When Tipha, Zakef, or Segol need to be subdivided and they have one or two Tevirs, Revi'a is used as the Divider.

רְבִיעַ

מֵקַּף רְבִיעַ

רְבִיעַ מֵרְכָא | מַהְפַּךְ

מֵרְכָא רְבִיעַ מֵרְכָא

Common Patterns

גֶּרֶשׁ

If a Tevir, Pashta, Revi'a or Zarka needs to be subdivided, the subdivider is usually Geresh or Gershayim.

גֶּרֶשׁ

גֵּרֵשׁ אַזְלָא
(a.k.a. קַדְמָא וְאַזְלָא)

אַזְלָא גֵּרֵשׁ

אַזְלָא גֵּרֵשׁ קַדְמָא פַּשְׁטָא–מֻנַּח
מֵקַּף גֵּרֵשׁ

Common Patterns

יְתִיב

מֵחַבֵּר יְתִיב

מֵחַבֵּר מֵרְכָא יְתִיב

פַּשְׁטָא יְתִיב (rare)

יְתִיב

Pashta is only used on the last or second-last syllable of a word. If a Pashta is needed on the first syllable, we use Yetiv, instead. Yetiv never uses a Link.

Common Patterns

גֵּרְשַׁיִם

מֵרְכָא גֵּרְשַׁיִם

גֵּרְשַׁיִם

If a Tevir, Pashta, Revi'a or Zarka needs to be subdivided, the subdivider is usually Geresh or Gershayim.

HAFTARAH TROP

Common Patterns

מֵֽהְפָּ֑ךְ פָּשֵׁ֫א

כֵּ֤ן דָּ֖

פָּשֵׁ֫א-גְּד֖וֹלָה֨

When Tevir, Revi'a, Pashta, or Zarka need to be subdivided, Telishah-Gedolah is sometimes used. When the accent is not on the first syllable, a second Telishah-Gedolah is often added to mark the stress. Telishah-Gedolah can be linked to up to six Munahs.

Common Patterns

מֵֽהְפָּ֑ךְ פָּזֵ֡ר

כֵּ֤ן דָּ֖

פָּ֜

 דָּ֖

פָּזֵ֡ר

Pazer is used to subdivide Tevir, Revi'a, Pashta, and Zarka. Pazer can be linked to up to six Munahs.

67

D'VAR TORAH WRITING GUIDE

This guide is intended to give you a general idea of what a typical D'var Torah looks like. Yours may not look exactly like this — it will, of course, be written by you and not me! — but it should include all of these elements. As always, make sure you consult with your rabbi / teacher.

1. Don't thank people for coming — that's something you can tell your guests at the party afterwards. The person giving the D'var Torah is called a *Darshan* — literally, an "explainer". The congregation will thank *you* for explaining the weekly readings to *them*.

2. In one or two paragraphs, summarize the content of the Torah and Haftarah readings for that day.

3. Quote a verse or idea from the Torah and/or Haftarah in Hebrew and in English, and discuss its relevance in our times. This is when you bring in your own commentaries and tell us what you've learned from our ancient and modern teachers.

4. Explain how the idea you've chosen has meaning to you. You can discuss the impact the D'var Torah may have had on how you're going to lead your life, how it's affected your commitment to Judaism and its values, etc.

5. If it fits with your ideas, you may want to talk about your parents, grandparents or other family members and role models and what positive values or lessons you've learned from them. Note: this is not the same as thanking them. Save the "thank you's" for after the service!

6. Final thoughts: what does becoming a Bar/Bat Mitzvah mean to you? Why is it special to you and what have you learned in the process of studying for today? Typically, this is where you bring your discussion back to the original idea you chose from the Torah / Haftarah.

7. Your D'var Torah should be no more than four or five double-spaced pages — roughly the length of a five to seven minute speech.

My **parashah**, book from the Torah, and chapter/verse

My **Haftarah** book and chapter/verse reference...

What the TORAH says in my own words:

What the HAFTARAH says in my own words:

Questions I have about my TORAH reading, Haftarah, Bar/Bat Mitzvah process, or Judaism in general (minimum 3):	Questions my parents have about my TORAH reading, Haftarah, Bar/Bat Mitzvah process, or Judaism in general (minimum 3):

SECTIONS OF TORAH THAT STAND OUT FOR ME...

Chapter : Verse OR Section	What it says in my own words	Why it stands out for me

SECTIONS OF HAFTARAH THAT STAND OUT FOR ME…

Chapter : Verse OR Section	What it says in my own words	Why it stands out for me
↑	↑	
↑	↑	
↑	↑	

One idea or theme I want to talk about (based on my choices from charts 3 and 4):	
Verse or section from the Torah or Haftarah that relates to my theme (choose 1 or 2 from charts 3 and/or 4 and write them here):	

Commentator	The commentator's own words	What I think the commentator is trying to teach
↑	↑	↑
↑	↑	↑
↑	↑	↑

One idea or theme I want to talk about:
(copy from previous chart)

Verse or section from the Torah or Haftarah that relates to my theme:
(copy from previous chart)

Commentator (copy from previous chart)	**What I think the commentator is trying to teach** (copy from previous chart)	**How this teaching relates to my life or the world around me**
↑	↑	↑
↑	↑	↑
↑	↑	↑

One idea or theme I want to talk about:

(copy from previous chart)

Verse or section from the Torah or Haftarah that relates to my theme:

(copy from previous chart)

My lesson for this *parashah* (bring all your ideas together)

Commentator (copy from previous chart)	How this teaching relates to my life or the world around me (copy from previous chart)

INCREDIBLY HANDY TIME LINE

The dates here are approximate. The two main columns compare the Tana<u>h</u>'s chronology with samples of writings from ancient Yisra'el's neighbors that relate to events in the Tana<u>h</u>. There are also thousands of Hebrew inscriptions and documents dug up by archeologists, but unfortunately I don't have space to mention them all! The narrow column on the left shows you when the books of the Torah and *Nevi'im* (Prophets) <u>take place</u>, **not** <u>when they were written</u>. See if you can locate your own Torah / Haftarah readings on this time line!

WHEN TORAH BOOKS TAKE PLACE	TIME LINE FROM THE TANAH (TORAH & PROPHETS ONLY)		STUFF WRITTEN ABOUT YISRA'EL BY YISRA'EL'S NEIGHBORS
BERESHIT	First Jewish family: Avraham, Sarah, Yitz<u>h</u>ak, Rivkah, Ya'akov, Le'ah, Ra<u>h</u>el, Yosef and all his brothers	1600 BCE 3600 years ago	
		1500 BCE 3500 years ago	
	Benay Yisra'el in Mitzra'im	1400 BCE 3400 years ago	
		1300 BCE 3300 years ago	
SHEMOT, VAYIKRA, BAMIDBAR, DEVARIM	Time of Moshe and the Exodus	1200 BCE 3200 years ago	Egyptian Pharaoh Merneptah records a list of nations living in Cana'an. "Yisra'el" is included in the list (1205 BCE)
	Benay Yisra'el capture land of Yisra'el		

When Navi Books Take Place				
YEHOSHU'A, SHOFTIM	Benay Yisra'el in Mitzra'im Time of Moshe and the Exodus Benay Yisra'el capture the land of Yisra'el and settle it. Time of the *Shoftim* (tribal chiefs).	**1200 BCE** 3200 years ago **1100 BCE** 3100 years ago	Egyptian Pharaoh Merneptah records a list of nations living in Cana'an. "Yisra'el" is included in the list (1205 BCE)	
SHEMU'EL	Time of King Sha'ul, King David and King Shlomo; First Temple is built; Kingdom of Yisra'el established	**1000 BCE** 3000 years ago		
I MELAHIM	Kingdom splits into Yehudah and Yisra'el (922 BCE) Book of *I Melahim* describes invasion of Yehudah by Pharaoh Shishak	**900 BCE** 2900 years ago	Egyptian Pharaoh Shishak writes a victory monument about invading the region in and around Yisra'el	
2 MELAHIM, AMOS, HOSHE'A, NAHUM, MICAH, YISH'AYAH #1	Time of Eliyahu and Elisha; Book of *2 Melahim* describes a rebellion against Yisra'el by Mesha, king of Mo'ab; *2 Melahim* also describes war between Aram, Yehudah, and Yisra'el	**800 BCE** 2800 years ago	King Mesha of Mo'ab makes a stone monument describing his rebellion against Israel; Anonymous king of Aram makes a stone monument describing war with Yehudah & Yisra'el	
	Ashur conquers Yisra'el (722-720 BCE) Books of *2 Melahim* and *Yish'ayah* describe Assyrian invasions of Yehudah and Yisra'el	**700 BCE** 2700 years ago	Assyrian kings Tiglath-Pileser III and Shalmaneser V write inscriptions and wall carvings about conquering Israel; Assyrian king Sennacherib writes inscription about his invasion of Yehudah	
2 MELAHIM, TZEFANYAH, YIRMIYAH, YEHEZKEL, YISH'AYAH #2, OVADYAH	**Bavel conquers Yehudah (590's-586 BCE)** Yerushalayim destroyed (586 BCE)	**600 BCE** 2600 years ago	**Babylonians write inscriptions about their invasion and conquest of Yehudah**	
HAGAI, ZEHARYAH, HABAKUK, MAL'AHI	Cyrus of Persia allows exiles to return from Bavel; Temple rebuilt; time of Nehemiyah & Ezra	**500 BCE** 2500 years ago	Persia conquers Babylon; Persian King Cyrus II writes inscription about his policy of allowing all exiled people to return home	

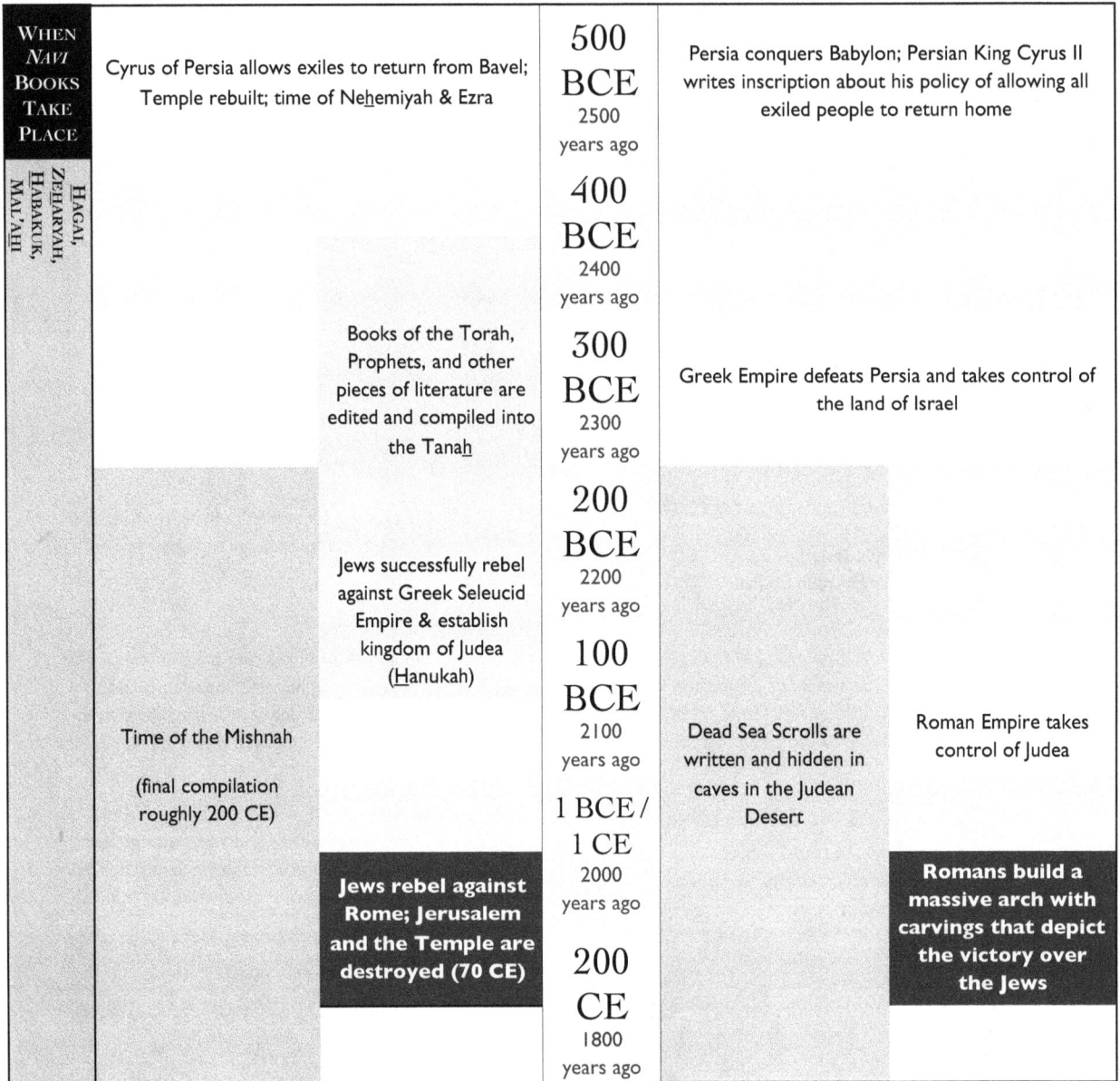

WHEN *NAVI* BOOKS TAKE PLACE				
HAGAI, ZEHARYAH, HABAKUK, MAL'AHI	Cyrus of Persia allows exiles to return from Bavel; Temple rebuilt; time of Nehemiyah & Ezra	**500 BCE** 2500 years ago		Persia conquers Babylon; Persian King Cyrus II writes inscription about his policy of allowing all exiled people to return home
		400 BCE 2400 years ago		
	Books of the Torah, Prophets, and other pieces of literature are edited and compiled into the Tanah	**300 BCE** 2300 years ago		Greek Empire defeats Persia and takes control of the land of Israel
	Jews successfully rebel against Greek Seleucid Empire & establish kingdom of Judea (Hanukah)	**200 BCE** 2200 years ago		
		100 BCE 2100 years ago		
Time of the Mishnah (final compilation roughly 200 CE)			Dead Sea Scrolls are written and hidden in caves in the Judean Desert	Roman Empire takes control of Judea
	Jews rebel against Rome; Jerusalem and the Temple are destroyed (70 CE)	**1 BCE / 1 CE** 2000 years ago		**Romans build a massive arch with carvings that depict the victory over the Jews**
		200 CE 1800 years ago		

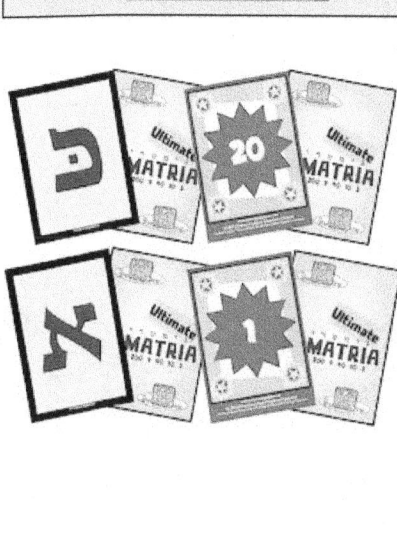

Ease your way into learning the Trop for Torah and Haftarah!

Our Trop Flashcards enhance any Bar/Bat Mitzvah study program. 28 5"x7" flashcards feature:

- the position of each ta'am in a word
- explanations that let you know what each ta'am is used for
- the most common patterns for each ta'am
- handy music charts
- a color-coding system to help students visualize the music
- suggestions for use
- terribly convenient explanatory notes and charts

Each set also includes a 12-page booklet that explains how the Trop system works.

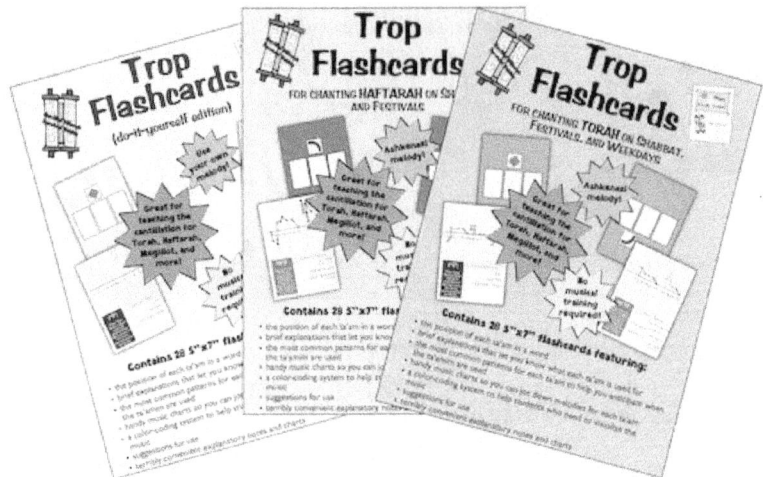

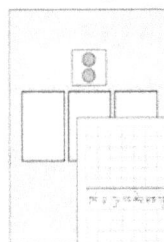

Zakef-Katon card, Do-It-Yourself edition (front and back sides).

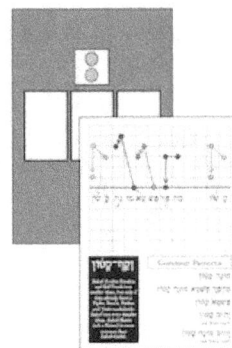

Zakef-Katon card, Haftarah edition (front and back sides).

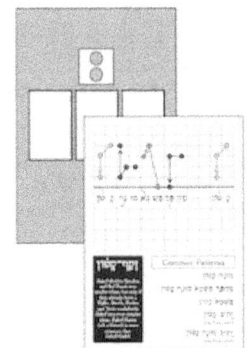

Zakef-Katon card, Torah edition (front and back sides).

Trop Poster Set

Excellent companion for teaching Trop to groups of any size!

Use the posters on their own or with our Trop Flashcards, Bar/Bat Mitzvah Survival Guides, or Ultimate Torah Trainer!

Contains 3 12"x18" posters:

- the Disjunctive ta'amim and when they're used
- the Conjunctive ta'amim and when they're used
- how ta'amim are used to divide a verse into segments

Simple explanations and examples!

The set also includes this handy explanation booklet!

Disjunctive Ta'amim: Dividers and their Levels

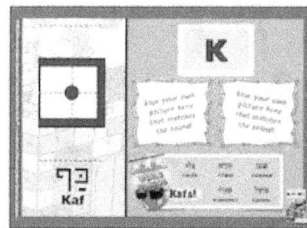

A fun way to learn about the Holy Days and the order of the Hebrew months!

The Hebrew months and Holy Days come alive with the Ḥagim & Ḥodashim Cards series. Meet any classroom or programming need with our large display cards, flashcards for small groups, or playing cards for active learning through games. Use them for:

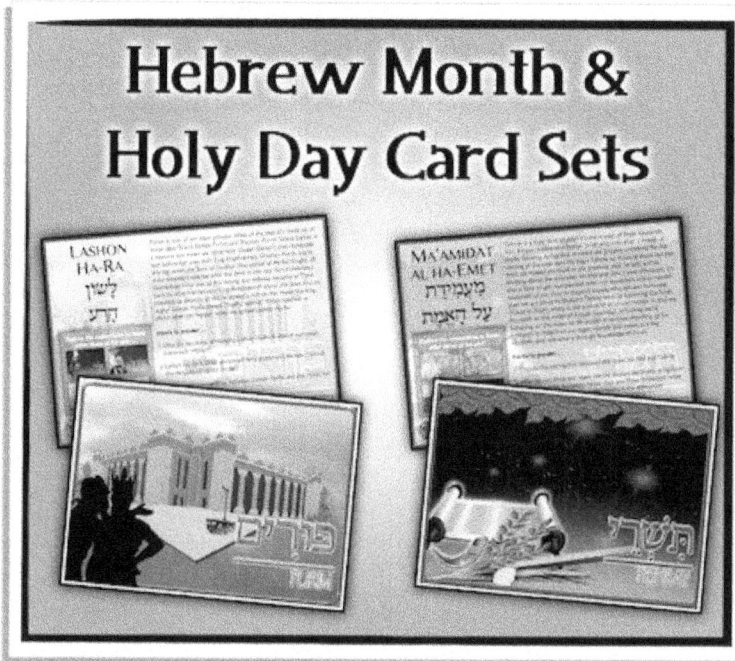

✓ Learning the order of the Hebrew months and Holy Days

✓ Connecting months and events in the year to Jewish values

✓ Designing a values-based program for the year

✓ And more!

Hebrew Month & Holy Day Card Sets

The 11"x8" display cards are perfect for word walls, sorting games, class displays, and more.

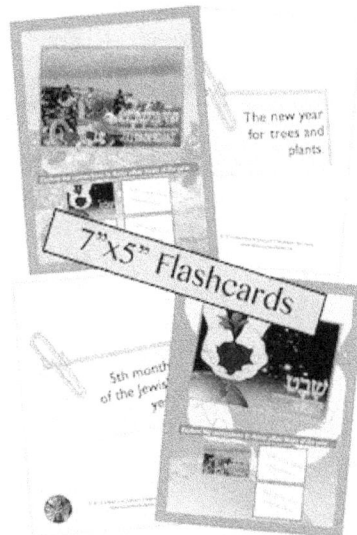

The 7"x5" flashcards are great for working with small groups.

The 4"x3" playing cards are great for match games, fish, memory games, and more. Suggestions for games are included.

www.ingramcontent.com/pod-product-compliance
Lightning Source LLC
Chambersburg PA
CBHW081240020426
42331CB00013B/3239

9 780987 780911